SMALL STEPS TO RICH 2022

Personal Finance Made Simple

KENNETH JEFFREY MARSHALL

ISBN 978-1-737-67340-8 (paperback)

Small Steps to Rich books are available at special quantity discounts when purchased in bulk for premiums, sales promotions, and client gifts. Special editions, including books with customized covers, corporate logos, and tailored forewords can also be created. For more information please visit www.smallstepstorich.com.

CONTENTS

PREFACE

What is *rich*?

To me, it's *the ability to make any reasonable choice without material financial penalty*.

It's when a loved one needs help, or the perfect home comes on the market, or a worthy cause wants your backing; and you can jump on it with justified confidence. It's securing what's important, seamlessly, and without fear.

So there's a lot that rich is *not* about. It's not about bling. It's not about being waited on hand and foot. It's not about invoking the envy of others.

It's about *freedom*. I'll share a personal example.

Some years I spend time traveling. But winters I'm always back in California. I grew up there, and these days teach at Berkeley during the first quarter.

Typical was 2016. On New Year's Day my plane touched down at SFO, and I moved back into my place near campus. It was close to my parents, old friends, and one of my sisters and her family. It was a good setup. Plus I just plain like Berkeley, as one might a peculiar aunt. Not by chance is it nicknamed *Bezerkeley*.

At the end of March I started a trip, as scheduled. I had intended to be away for several months. But in early May mom called. Dad—who had been unwell—had just received a bad diagnosis. Apparently he had only half a year left to live. So I flew back.

That's it.

I didn't have to plead for time off. I didn't need to scour the web for a discount ticket. I didn't fear a demotion, loss of income, or any other economic hit. I didn't have to.

The reason I came back to California was sad. But the time I got to spend with dad was precious. He had accepted his situation, as eventually did I. So we could just be with each other. Nothing—no sincere praise, no honest good wish—was left unsaid between father and son.

Of course no sensible person would think of the fatal diagnosis of a parent as a gift. I certainly didn't. But to be called like that—to have circumstances summon you to something that truly matters, and to be free to drop everything for it—

That, to me, is rich.

And it's attainable. The steps to rich turn out to be small.

But unfortunately, they're rarely taught. Personal finance isn't baked into our schooling.

There have, however, been attempts to make it so. For example in 1985—just in time for my graduation, ironically—my state began requiring a high school economics course. The hope was that the next generation of Californians would emerge better equipped to handle money issues, from mortgages to mutual funds.

That hasn't happened. The course now focuses more on comparative systems—like socialism versus capitalism—than on basics like credit scores, automatic bill pay, and high-yield online savings accounts.

Some other states have made more headway. Six now require a standalone personal finance course: Alabama, Iowa, North Carolina, Tennessee, Utah, and Virginia. Fifteen more include personal finance lessons in other courses.[1] But that still leaves a lot of Americans out. Most high school graduates just get thrown to the money wolves.

Plus the personal finance courses that are offered sometimes fall short. Their curriculums can be counterproductive. A good example is the stock picking competition. It has students take a stab at which stocks will close higher at the end of the semester. But that's often just a dozen weeks away. That's far too short a period for any sensible investment thesis to play out. The timetable is inconsistent with the endeavor, like speed sleeping. The lesson winds up encouraging precisely the wrong behavior: guessing.

So if you've been flummoxed by money choices, please remember this: *it's not your fault.* Our education system failed you. It saw personal finance as a diversion, not an essential. It left your training in the hands of credit card companies, fund managers, and insurance agents. Well-intentioned though those folks may be, they have conflicts of interest. Your edification is not their goal.

This all dawned on me while I was teaching value investing at Stanford. It bugged me. So in 2020 I created a personal finance course. The notes for that course became this book.

But this isn't some esoteric college text. It's practical. It's written to be used, like a wrench is made to turn bolts. Absent is the Wall Street jargon and Greek letter formulas that, candidly, aren't particularly illuminating anyway.

A good example of this is the glossary. It's frank. I've tried to keep each definition to under 20 words. That's because when you hear *market cap*, all you need to know is that that means *price for all the stock*. How that may depend on convertible debentures and unexercised warrants—don't ask—isn't critical.

For my devotion to succinctness I expect a hailstorm of abuse from the financial priesthood. Macroeconomists will ridicule my rudimentary explanation of *inflation*. Estate lawyers will blast my elementary take on *trusts*. Investment advisors will mock my romp through *volatility*.

I also expect barbs for my summary dismissal of whole categories of financial products. These include *annuities*, *hedge funds*, and *whole life insurance*. I boot them all in just a few lines.

But that's the right thing to do. Those products are helpful so infrequently that they're just not worth studying.

So to any overpaid sharks that feel threatened by my straight shooting, I say, *so what?* This isn't a dissertation, and they're not my audience. You are. And you certainly have better things to do than to wade through inessential gobbledygook.

While gobbledygook may be absent, subjectivity is not. That's because this book is entirely my opinion. It reflects my views, my distillation of what I see as best practices. The subject matter makes that a necessity. So please read every sentence as if it started with *my opinion is*.

Another limiting necessity is geography. This book is meant for U.S. citizens and residents. That's because almost immediately we get into quirks of the American system, from *IRAs* to the *FDIC*. Such references would ring hollow for people outside of the U.S., just like *superannuation*—an Australian retirement program —and *ISKs*—a Swedish investment account—would fall flat with Americans.

Some other books take a more global approach. But my sense is that our focus results in a more actionable program.

That said, some of those other books are great. Their advice is specific and excellent. *Spend less than you earn. Cut up your credit card. Pay your bills early.* I celebrate that some people need to read only them to establish healthy habits.

But for many people, they don't work. They ring hollow. They read like user manuals for gadgets whose utility isn't evident. This book attacks that by starting with the *why*. It lays down the mental underpinnings of personal finance mastery. It recognizes that tips are more likely to resonate when it's made clear at the outset why they work.

That resonance is crucial. It's crucial because it sits at the foundation of *your* ability to make any reasonable choice without material financial penalty.

And those choices are coming. You've got a slate of upcoming life events—some wonderful and some challenging, but all vital—that are counting on your unconditional availability.

ACKNOWLEDGMENTS

Value investing—the subject of my first book—is an idiosyncratic pursuit. Most folks don't give a hoot about it. So when I needed advice in writing *Good Stocks Cheap*, I had a limited universe of friends to call upon.

Not so with personal finance. It's not just for freaks like me who think nothing of spending Saturday night curled up with a good annual report. Unlike value investing, personal finance is for everybody.

I mention this because readers may notice that there's little overlap between the people acknowledged in the first book and in this one. That's not because the first lot abandoned me, I assure you. It's because I made full use of the universality of personal finance to reach out to a broader range of acquaintances. They included a New Hampshire engineer, a California architect, a Michigan lawyer, and an Oregon bibliophile. Without complaint this able squad cheerfully proofread, opined, and supported. My sincere thanks to all of them:

> Julie Canner, Margaret Cohen, Jakob Diepenbrock, Allison Joyce, Philip Leiser, Michael McDonnell, Jack Morris, Star Pesetsky, Kristin Ring, Audrey Skinner, Tom Svedenstrand, Wolfgang Wagener, and John Yannone;

> At Stanford University, Teresa Kpachavi and Emma Walker for greenlighting and marketing my personal finance course;

> And dear mother. That the apple of my father's eye had a master's degree in English has turned out to be of inordinate use to the product of that union.

If this work rings true it is the above heroes to whom you are obliged. But where it falls short it is but I—earnest yet flawed—that is to blame.

INTRODUCTION

This book puts forth a model. It's a model for mastering personal finance.

The model is—foremost—simple. It's simple because when done right, personal finance is simple.

Done wrong, it's complicated. So the model isn't plain just to make it easier to learn, although that is a result. It's plain because that's what works best. In keeping our approach straightforward, we sacrifice *nothing*.

The model has three steps: *think*, *see*, and *do*.

First is *think.* Think is about mindset. It's about the uncommon way that those on their way to wealth consider things. They make financial decisions with a healthy mental orientation that most others never seek. That orientation is the bedrock of their good moves. It naturally yields smart money choices. More importantly, it blocks bad ones.

Second is *see*. With a rich mindset, you'll see clearly the different spheres of personal finance. There are seven: *working, spending, borrowing, saving, investing, insuring,* and *planning*. You'll start to view splurges as corrosive, debt as entrapment, saving as calming, and investing as painless. It will be as if you finally got eyeglasses with the right prescription after having worn the wrong ones for years.

Third is *do*. With a rich mindset and the correct views, it will become obvious what actions to take. The wise moves will become intuitive. More importantly, the destructive ones will become revolting. You'll reject them automatically, as you might the prospect of vacationing in a gym locker.

The three steps of the model are sequential. They build on each other. So each should be grasped before moving on. If the proper mindset isn't adopted, the seven spheres of personal finance won't be seen correctly. If the seven spheres aren't seen correctly, the right actions won't be taken.

That makes the first step fundamental. *Think* lays the groundwork for everything else. But it's also the hardest to absorb. That's because it deals with how we feel about things. So those chapters may seem soft. Unnecessary, even. After all, you weren't poking around for a book in the psychology section.

But *think* is essential. It's the root of all that follows.

I do not assume that personal finance fascinates you. Instead, I assume that you view it as you might a dentist appointment: unpleasurable, yet constructive. I may personally be riveted by the history of municipal bonds—it's nonstop thrills here at the Marshall house—but you're probably not into such things. Instead, you just want personal finance *handled.*

So I've skipped nonessentials. The main nonessential that's missing is a mainstay of many personal finance books: how to muddle along. It's about navigating the sewers: surfing teaser rates from one usurious credit card to another, skirting bankruptcy, and buying private mortgage insurance because of a puny down payment on a home.

Those aren't steps to rich. They're steps to mediocre. They're financial cesspools, and they're not for us. What is for us is *winning.*

I appreciate how rah-rah that sounds. But attitude matters. Folks who focus on the economy's miserable options tend to gobble them up. But people who focus on the steps to rich tend to climb them.

So focus on the steps. Focus on the steps because in 2022 America you really do have to know this stuff. The laws that should protect you from underqualified advisors, aggressive lenders, and unscrupulous marketers are either unenacted, unenforced, or weak. You're on your own.

Focus also because you can't just outsource everything to a financial planner. Even the best ones have motivations that diverge from yours. Plus there are aspects of your economic life that they can't monitor.

It's like nutrition. You can hire a nutritionist. But ultimately it's you that sticks things in your mouth.

In this book I refer to several financial institutions by name. I do this to provide substantial examples, and to introduce you to some companies that you might find useful. But please know that I haven't been paid or otherwise encouraged to promote any of them. In the rare case that I own stock in one of them, I'll disclose that.

The companies worth mentioning can change. So make sure that this is the most recent edition of this book. That way you'll know about the companies that are relevant today, as well as the rules, interest rates, and tax brackets that matter now.

Also, please read the whole book before taking action. It's just easier to prioritize after you have the whole picture. Something that seems urgent after chapter 10 may emerge as deferrable by chapter 23. So take it all in before deciding what to do first.

But don't expect results overnight. While some moves can pay off quickly—like those around *select*, the topic of chapter 18—most take time to flower. Ours is a long-term practice whose merits take decades to play out.

But play out they do. Few subjects are as masterable, and as potent, as personal finance. It's masterable because it's straightforward. And it's potent because it has the power to level up your life.

Rich may not be your goal. The ability to make any reasonable choice without material financial penalty may be more than you need. You may be perfectly satisfied with *plenty*.

But *rich* is still your heading. That's because *rich* and *plenty* are points on the same vector. Rich is just further out. It's direction, if not destination, that's reflected in the title. Perhaps it could have been more modest. But there just wasn't much punch in *Small Steps to Sufficient*.

CHAPTER 1

SCALE

How important is it that you put this book to work? That depends. It depends on where you currently sit on the personal finance scale. The scale has five stages.

No one is judging you here. The scale just lets you check, privately, where you're starting from.

Stage five is the most urgent. It's characterized by *overspending*, *indebtedness*, and a *negative net worth*. Each of those three terms merits some clarification.

Overspending is consuming more than net income. Gauging it is easy.

Start by estimating your average annual expenses. Just look at your last 12 months of costs. Add up all of your credit card charges, debit card charges, cash payments—everything. Don't exclude something just because it seems like a one-off. It happened, and that's sufficient. When in doubt, overestimate.

Next, check your annual net income. That's the amount of cash you receive from work, dividends, interest, Social Security, and anything else, after any withheld taxes. Just look at the last 12 months of inflows to your bank account. Then, add in any cash you received but didn't deposit.

If that total is less than annual expenses, that's overspending.

Indebtedness is the state of owing money. *Any* money. That includes debts that charge interest, like a student loan or a mortgage. But it also includes interest-free debts like loans from friends or family, as well as credit card debt with a temporary zero percent teaser rate.

A *negative net worth* means that *liabilities* exceed *assets*. Liabilities are all amounts owed. It equals all debt plus any unpaid bills from vendors, like a cable company; and agencies, like the IRS. Assets equal anything you own that has a readily ascertainable value, like a bank account, a car, or a home.

If you're at stage five—if you overspend, are indebted, and have a negative net worth— you're in luck. That's because you'll get more out of this book than most. But understand that this book should now become a priority. Please put it to work for you at once.

Stage four is also urgent, but less so. It too has the characteristics of overspending and indebtedness. But it features a *positive* net worth. Assets exceed liabilities. That's better. Stage four nonetheless still requires attention because overspending and indebtedness can gang up to beat net worth back into negative territory.

Stage three still suffers from indebtedness. But it has the positive net worth of stage four, plus *under*spending. Consumption is less than net income. Now we're getting somewhere.

Stage two's hallmarks are underspending, no debt, and positive net worth. At this stage the goal is not to stabilize a bad situation, but to improve a good one.

Stage one features underspending, no debt, and *high* net worth. It's where you're headed.

Admittedly, the distinctions between the five stages are blurry. For example, where does a *positive* net worth become a *high* net worth? As of 2022 I'd say somewhere between $1,000,000 and $2,000,000. It depends on one's lifestyle and location, in my view. But your number could be outside of that range and just as valid.

Plus there's indebted, and there's *indebted*. It's one thing to owe $500, and another thing to owe $500,000.

In short, the personal finance scale has its imprecisions. But it's still useful. It's useful because it gives you the honest read you need to start. It lets you identify your situation. And once you've identified it, you can master it.

SUMMARY

The five stages on the personal finance scale, in order if increasing severity, are:

1. Stage one: Underspending, no debt, and a high net worth
2. Stage two: Underspending, no debt, and a positive net worth
3. Stage three: Underspending, indebted, and a positive net worth
4. Stage four: Overspending, indebted, and a positive net worth
5. Stage five: Overspending, indebted, and a negative net worth

PART I

THINK

CHAPTER 2

ODDS

Think

Odds

People on their way to wealth think differently.

Not because they have high IQs, or because they went to fancy schools. Those things don't matter. They think differently because they chose to adopt a rich mindset.

Somewhere along the way they picked up particularly useful mental models. It could have been from a parent, from a friend's family, or just from reading. However they did it, they got the ability to think with clarity about the different aspects of economic life.

Odds, for example.

Some things are likely to happen. Sunrise, say. Tomorrow morning, the sun is likely to rise. It's always done so, and the basics of the skies seem to remain intact. So it will probably rise again. In fact, it's so probable that we count on it.

Sunrises can vary, of course. Sometimes they can be hard to see, because of clouds. Other times they happen later than they did the day before, as the seasons change. But just because sunrises are sometimes hard to see, or later, we don't pretend that they stopped happening. We still count on them, and rightly so.

That's *odds*. Formally, it's called *probability*. We plan on the sun rising because the overwhelming odds are that it will.

In personal finance, odds rule. They govern outcomes. Smart people harness this fact to advantage by letting odds show them what to count on.

Inflation, for example. People on their way to wealth count on it. Prices go up. Not in every year, not in every country, and not in every product category. But generally, prices rise. For proof, consider my boyhood adventures with ice cream.

Ah, the Balboa Bar. It's a block of vanilla ice cream on a stick first dunked in a pot of molten chocolate, and then caked with crushed peanuts on one side and chocolate sprinkles on the other. If my Southern California youth had any perfections, this was it.

I bought my first Balboa Bar in the summer of 1979 for $1.25. Forty-one years later in 2021, I bought one for $4.50. That comes out to an annual average price increase of around 3 percent. Put differently, the money required to buy one Balboa Bar in 1979 bought only a *quarter* of one in 2021. Time beat back the purchasing power of the dollar.

As it turns out, the Balboa Bar nicely approximates inflation generally. Between 1979 and 2021 U.S. inflation also averaged around 3 percent per year.[1]

That inflation happened makes sense. It makes sense because the world's population grew. Between 1979 and 2021, it almost doubled. That meant more people wanting more things. Many of those things couldn't be made fast enough to satisfy growing demand. So the price of those things rose. That's inflation. And since the population seems to still be growing, the odds are that it will continue.

Another way odds rule personal finance is with *returns*. A return is money made on an investment.

Consider money returning 1 percent per year. One percent is what one might earn, after taxes, on a normal savings account at a bank. Some years it's higher. Other years it's lower, perhaps even zero. And the rates vary by country. But one percent is a sensible approximation.

Now instead think about money growing at 7 percent. Seven percent is what one might earn after taxes from a low-cost stock index fund. Some years it would be higher. Other years it would be lower, maybe even negative. And again, it would vary by country. More on all of that later.

What's useful to note now is that the stock fund's 7 percent is higher than the bank account's 1 percent. *Much* higher. And therein lies the likelihood: the odds are that over time and on average, returns from a low-cost stock index fund will be higher than returns from a bank savings account.

Sometimes this can be hard to believe. Take 2018. That year the returns from major stock index funds were less than those from bank savings accounts. In 2018 the S&P 500 Total Return—a standard index that we'll visit later—returned -4.4 percent. That's *negative* four point four percent. It went *down*. By contrast, an account at MySavingsDirect—an online savings option of the sort that we'll also cover later—returned 1.8 percent. So that year, cash beat stocks. It also did in 2008, and in 2002.

But those years were like sunrises obscured by clouds. They tried to disguise a likely event as an unlikely one. But people with a rich mindset weren't fooled. They know that the odds are that stocks will outperform other kinds of assets over their lifetimes.

Incidentally, this does not mean that we should pour all of our wealth into low-cost stock index funds. As we'll see later, cash has some merits that stocks don't.

Stocks are an *asset class*. An asset class is a group of things you can own that have similar characteristics.

Stocks are ownership stakes in businesses. They can be *public*, meaning listed on a stock exchange; or *private*, as with ownership stakes in startups. When we talk about indexes like the S&P 500 Total Return, we're talking about *public* stocks.

Cash is another kind of asset class. Dollars, pounds, and rupees all belong to the asset class called cash.

Yet a different asset class is *bonds*. Bonds are borrowings by governments and companies. They promise to pay interest; as well as to repay principal, or the amount that the government or company originally borrowed.

The relative performance of these three asset classes has been remarkably persistent. Cash returned modestly, bonds returned better, and stocks—public stocks—returned best. And since little has fundamentally changed, the odds are that this will continue.

STOCKS

BONDS

CASH

Another way odds rule personal finance is with *indexes*. There are funds you can invest in that are tied to an index like the S&P 500 Total Return. They're managed *passively*—that is, they just own exactly what's in the index. So predictably, these funds perform like the index on which they're based.

Other funds are managed *actively*. They don't own the index. Instead, they own specific stocks that their managers figured should do particularly well. Many individuals try this too, actively trading in and out of stock positions.

Active managers mean well. But on average and over time, they fail. The index—also called *the market*—trounces them. The odds simply favor passive management.

To be clear, there will always be exceptional periods. There will be years when inflation is zero, when bank accounts beat stock index funds, and when actively managed stock funds beat the market. But those are infrequent. And when they happen, they don't happen with such force that they upset the odds laid out here.

There will also be exceptional cases. Take *angel investing*. That's buying stock in private, unlisted startups. Most people lose money doing it. But some don't. They excel at it. They may have special connections or talents that enable them to achieve improbable results.

But again, those are not normal cases. They're rare. They really happened, but they're *outliers*. They're not *averages*. That's why people on their way to wealth don't count on them.

Odds matter more now than ever. That's because of longevity.

A hundred years ago I could expect to live until my early 50s. Such was life expectancy at the time. But today, that's just middle age.[2] Mere youth, I like to think.

With more years on earth, we're more likely to have financial results that match the odds. There's a greater chance now than there was a century ago that my stocks will return better than my cash. Stated differently, *odds become obvious over time*. And as we'll see, that's grounds for optimism. Not that living longer wasn't enough by itself.

SUMMARY

1. Odds govern results.
2. Over the long term, the odds are that prices will inflate, stocks will return more than bonds, bonds will return more than cash, and low-cost stock index funds will beat actively-managed stock funds.
3. The longer the period of time, the more relevant the odds.
4. Outliers and averages are different.

CHAPTER 3

RISK

Think

Odds
Risk

Risk is the chance of loss. Smart people minimize it.

This may be hard to believe. After all, don't people become rich by *taking* risks? And aren't stocks—the highest returning asset class—*risky*?

No. Risk is an area where common thinking is very different from rich thinking.

The easiest way to understand risk is to consider how one might *maximize* it. What would guarantee a loss? Three clever schemes come to mind.

One, overpay. Just buy an asset for vastly more than it's worth. That would make it hard to ever sell it for more than your cost, locking in a loss. *Voila.*

Two, need to sell. Put yourself in a position where you'll be forced to accept a lowball price for an asset that you own. Not necessarily when it was *worth* less—it could still be a perfectly fine holding—just when its price happened to be down.

A stock, for example. Publicly traded shares bop around in price all the time. Those minute-by-minute fluctuations reflect peoples' changing moods. Folks flit between panic and optimism, and stock prices mirror those swings. So if you happened to need cash at a moment when people thought ill of your stock, you'd be forced to sell at a loss. Perfect.

Three, get saddled with a massive expense. A medical bill, for example. In America, hospital charges can be outrageous. They're a routine cause of personal bankruptcy. And since the odds are that at some point you'll need health care, you could clinch a loss by being personally responsible for the bill.

Of course this whole exercise seems silly. Plotting out ways to maximize risk looks ridiculous. But it's actually fundamental to correct thinking. It's fundamental in two ways.

First, it's amazing to realize how some people do *exactly* these things. Some overpay for a house. Others shop so uncontrollably that they're forced to sell investments at low prices just to pay credit card bills. Still others go uninsured, increasing the odds that they'll have to shoulder some big future expense all by themselves.

Second, we can invert. We can think about how to maximize risk, and then do the opposite.

That's how smart people minimize risk. They do the opposite. They *don't* overpay. They *don't* put themselves in a position where they could be forced to sell an asset at a time that they didn't choose. And they *don't* go without essential insurance policies.

Please realize how straightforward this is. One considers how to maximize risk, and then inverts to minimize risk. It's simple.

Further, it makes three common notions of risk seem absurd.

First is the idea that risk equals *volatility*. Volatility measures how much an asset's market price has fluctuated. It's commonly equated with risk. Stocks again provide a good example.

Consider stocks in two different companies, A and B. Say that over the last year stock A moved in price between $20 and $30 per share. Stock B, by contrast, flitted between $10 and $40 per share. The latter is a bigger range. It shows greater volatility. So conventionally, stock B would be seen as riskier because its price fluttered around in a bigger space.

But what if company B was established, growing, and profitable? And what if company A was a perpetual money loser that was about to run out of cash? Those facts would certainly seem important. By contrast, volatility would seem trivial.

It may be *uncertain* what the price of stock B will do tomorrow, or next week, or even next year. But uncertainty and risk are different. While risk is the chance of loss, uncertainty is the chance of gain *or* loss. The former is feared, and rightly so. But as we'll see, the latter can be leveraged to advantage.

The second absurd notion is called the *risk-return trade-off*. It's the belief that higher potential returns come from accepting greater risk. But if risk is the chance of loss, it could never cause higher potential returns. How could a loss increase returns? It couldn't. That's why the rich mindset regards the risk-return trade-off as crazy.

Third is the notion that the stock market is inherently risky. Stock prices bop around a lot, yes. But contrast stocks with cash. While stocks are busy appreciating and paying dividends, cash gets the purchasing power beaten out of it by inflation.

If in 1979 I had put my $1.25 of ice cream money in the bank, by 2021 I could have bought only one-quarter of a Balboa Bar. If instead I had put it in a low-cost stock index fund, by 2021 I could have bought *four* Balboa Bars. Viewed that way, it's staying in cash that seems risky.

Cash has merit, to be sure. It's critical to hold some, as we'll see. But to invest in it—to hold it in pursuit of a high return—is nuts.

To be clear, there's always the occasional risky act that yields great results. There's the entrepreneur who maxes out a credit card to start a business that eventually thrives. There's the investor that buys stock in some flailing outfit that improbably turns itself around. And there's the homeowner that overpays for a condominium that eventually gets sold at a profit during a real estate bubble. Such stories get romanticized to the point that they seem almost virtuous.

But those stories aren't normal. That's why we know about them. They're *told.* Their exceptionality makes them newsworthy.

They're outliers, not averages. No sensible person would count on their recurrence. The odds are simply against it.

SUMMARY

1. Risk is the chance of loss.
2. Risk does not equal volatility.
3. Higher potential returns do not come from accepting greater risk.
4. Stocks are not inherently riskier than cash.
5. Smart people minimize risk by not overpaying, never needing to sell, and offloading big future expenses.

CHAPTER 4

GROWTH

Think

Odds
Risk
Growth

Money grows. It can grow bigger, or it can grow smaller.

That may all seem obvious. But what's not obvious is just how extreme that growth can be.

Consider the happy scenario of money growing bigger. Start with some amount. Your current bank balance, say. Now imagine that balance growing by 1 percent per year. Think about it doing that for 30 years.

It would look like this:

Left to right is years, from one to 30. And low to high is your bank balance. As expected, the balance grows a bit each year.

There's an important fact about that picture that may be hard to see. At first it looks like a straight line. But please look again. It's not a straight line. It's a curve. Try laying a ruler, or the edge of a sheet of printer paper, alongside it. Now you can see that it bends up. Each year it rises a little bit more than it did the year before.

That's because the 1 percent earned one year becomes part of the base on which the following year's 1 percent gets applied. So over time, the growth amplifies. The result is a balance that grows not steadily, but acceleratedly.

That's the power of *compounding.*

One percent isn't much, of course. And that's what makes the curve hard to see. So consider a higher rate. Seven percent, for example. Here's the balance growing for the same 30 years at 7 percent:

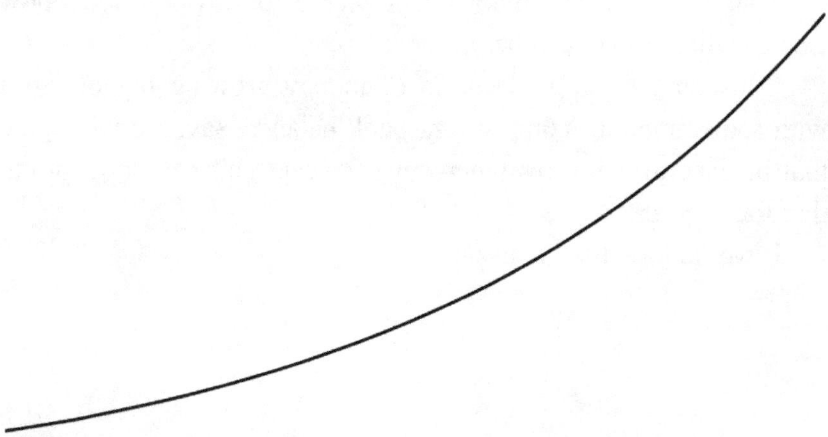

Now the curve is unmissable. And as we know, 7 percent isn't fiction. It's what one might earn on average after tax from a low-cost stock index fund.

There's another important fact about the curve that's worth noticing. Most of the increase happens *late*. Look again. After half of the years have passed—midway between left and right—the curve has grown to less than half of its eventual height. In fact, it's grown to less than a *third* of its eventual height:

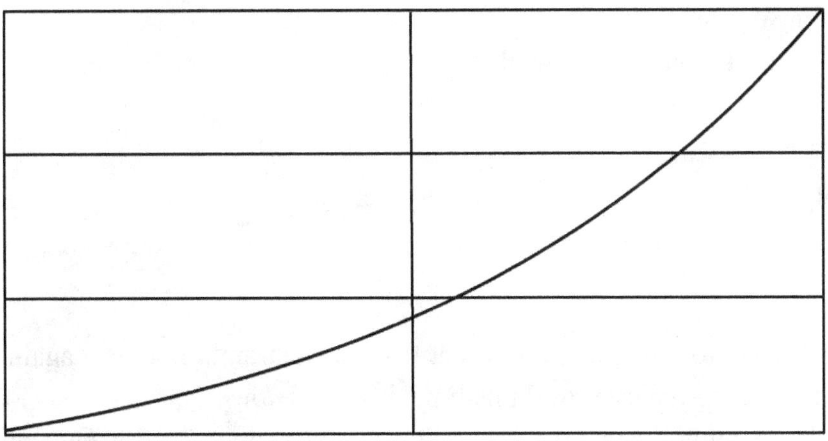

If the balance wasn't invested at all for the first 15 years, but instead grew at 7 percent for just the second 15 years, it would never get very high:

That's a much less impressive rise. The 15 year delay really stunts growth. That's because the big surge was never given a chance to happen.

In short, money grows bigger in *curves*. And that growth is extreme if it starts *early*.

Now consider the less pleasant case of money growing smaller. Think about money shrinking at a rate of 1 percent per year, again for 30 years.

That would look like this:

Here too the picture looks at first like a straight line. But again, it isn't. It's a curve. And this time, it curves *down*.

At higher rates, the curve down is alarming. Fifteen percent, for example:

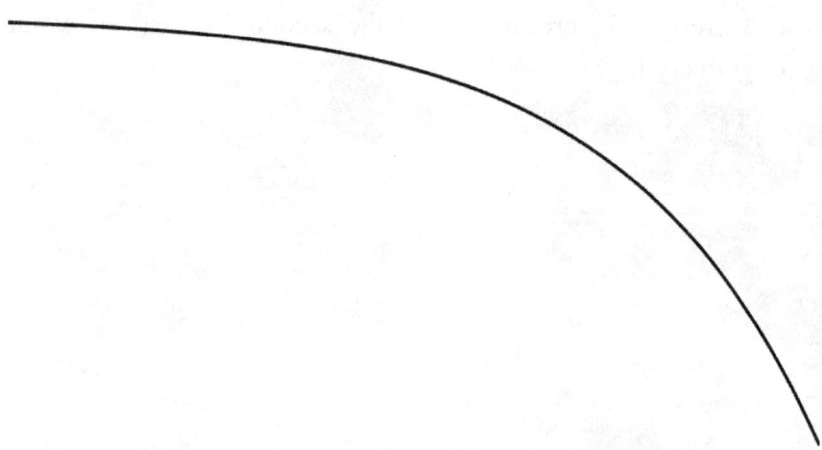

Again, the higher rate makes the curve unmissable. It's an increasingly steep plunge. And unfortunately, 15 percent isn't made up. It's real. As of this writing 15 percent is the approximate average interest rate charged on credit card debt.[1]

Compounding works negatively with the same force that it works positively. Outstanding credit card debt may cost 15 percent per year to carry. That's a lot. But the real cost comes from the addition of that 15 percent to next year's outstanding amount. That's why debt doesn't grow gradually. It explodes. It drives net worth down with a vengeance.

Smart people understand this. They think of money growth in curves, not lines. That's why they have such an easy time embracing the standard personal finance guidelines to start investing early, and to pay down debt promptly. It's why they can't shovel money into good investments fast enough, and why they extinguish debts as if they were the first flames of a house fire.

SUMMARY

1. Money grows bigger in curves.
2. Money also grows smaller in curves.
3. Growth—whether positive or negative—is extreme if it starts early.

CHAPTER 5

NEEDS

Think

Odds
Risk
Growth
Needs

We don't need much.

Somewhere to live, sure. Food. Clothes. We can also probably make good use of transportation, education, and medical care. But in the end, there's not that much that we truly need.

There's quite a bit that we *want*, however. We want a bigger house. We want vast wardrobes, food by the platterful, and cars with the horsepower of battleships.

Such wants are understandable. From all sides, we're urged to have them. Ads push us to live large. Social media pummels us with images of influencers luxuriating in finery. Stores seduce us into equating consumption with satisfaction. We're prompted to spend unthinkingly, liberally, and frequently.

Our history as a species drives our wants, too. Consider evolution. Our prehistoric ancestors improved their chance of survival by grabbing all the resources they could. Hoarding meant longevity. We inherited that instinct.

But the rich mindset separates needs and wants.

Needs help us to stay happily alive. They persist until they're fulfilled because they represent our real requirements.

By contrast, many wants are fleeting. They go away. They can be safely neglected. That's why smart people tag most wants as passing fancies best ignored.

There's even evidence that giving in to wants *causes* unhappiness. Troves of stuff become clutter that's hard to manage, cumbersome to sort through, and costly to maintain. Gluttony turns out to be boorish, not elegant.

Of course smart people with money buy plenty of things. They buy nice homes, clothes, and cars. But they're *discerning*. They're picky about what they consume. They *select*. They buy what they truly need, and some of what they truly like. But they don't gorge on all the goods and services that are offered to them. They know that an impulse to buy is not an order to act.

I've bought nice things. I've bought Italian suits, Olympic swim goggles, and vacations in nice villas. I'm looking out at the Pacific Ocean from the deck of one right now, actually.

But my Italian suit collection numbers only two. My Olympic swim goggles let me exercise comfortably and often. And the villas I rent let me spend meaningful time on holiday with family. Mine are not pointless expenditures made in passion. They're purposeful.

Correspondingly, there are a lot of things I don't buy. I've never owned a smartphone. I haven't owned a television since 1992.

My aversion to inessentials may seem extreme. And admittedly, sometimes it's absurd. For example, I actually haven't owned a wallet for about 20 years. I just stuff cards and bills in my pocket. What's wrong with that? Plenty, according to friends puzzled at my spilling everything out on the counter just to find the Visa card.

But one can still make use of the distinction between needs and wants without signing up for my severe brand of nothingness.

Consumption trends change. As of this writing, minimalism is in vogue. Time Magazine's 2019 Person of the Year advocates *stop shop*, a pledge to buy only items that are absolutely necessary.[1] Millennials—those born between 1981 and 1996—are less attracted to physical possessions than were earlier generations. Recent books on decluttering have become best-sellers.

The current interest in minimalism is sparked in part by climate change. Fewer products purchased means fewer products manufactured, which cuts down on emissions. It's also caused in part by memories of the 2008 financial crisis, when the price of houses plummeted. That caused many to stop seeing home purchases as paving stones on the road to financial freedom. But regardless of why it happened, the resurgence of minimalism makes the appeal of a needs-based spending policy more apparent.

Wants are dangerous because they first show up disguised as needs. But they become really dangerous when they actually *become* needs. This can happen because of addiction.

Many scientists agree that under certain circumstances people can come to need significant quantities of nicotine, alcohol, or other substances. Gambling also seems to be addictive. And all of these things cost money. So many smart people think of them as threats to their wealth.

Of course the main reason to avoid addiction isn't economic. It's health. Further, the logic of personal finance can never be enough to overcome an established addiction.

But it can make clear why it's useful to avoid addiction in the first place. It would increase one's needs. And no sensible person would opt to turn a harmful want into a compulsory, recurring expense.

SUMMARY

1. Needs and wants are different.
2. Our needs are few, but our wants are many.
3. Most wants are fleeting.
4. Gluttony is boorish, not elegant.
5. Addiction is the unhealthy expansion of needs.

CHAPTER 6

FADE

Think

Odds Fade
Risk
Growth
Needs

One more of something often disappoints.

Remember the Balboa Bar? Eating one is delightful. Messy, and delightful.

One could even imagine having two. In your service, I've tried this. The second packs a little less zing than the first, but it's still good.

Three, however, is pushing it. That's where the stomach ache kicks in. And a fourth wouldn't go over well at all. Beyond that one becomes a gastroenterological daredevil.

In other words, each additional Balboa Bar delivers less delight than did the last. The incremental satisfaction fades.

And so it goes for many products, from home square footage to amusement park visits. The pleasure derived from each successive unit goes down.

Economists call this *diminishing marginal utility*. Diminishing means fading. Marginal means additional. And utility means usefulness. The more we get of something, the less satisfying each one turns out to be.

It looks like this:

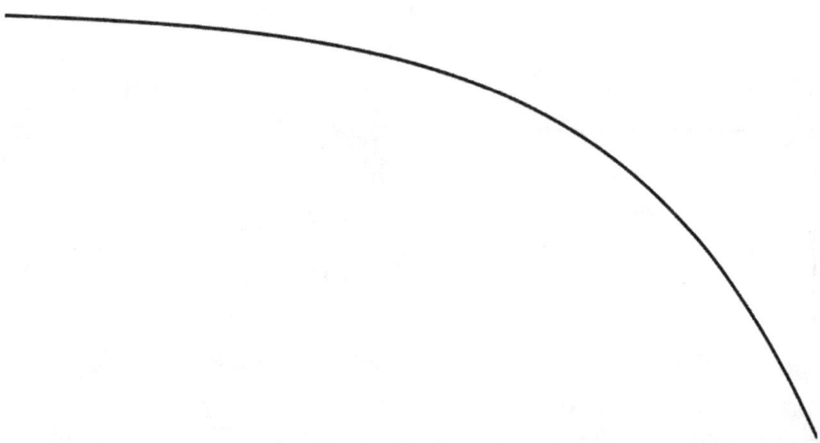

Left to right is the number of units: one Balboa Bar, two, three, and so on. Low to high is utility.

Sometimes an additional unit of something isn't just less satisfying. It's *worse*. If it's the third Balboa Bar that starts the stomach ache, then that's where the utility curve would drop below zero. The third Balboa Bar would have *negative marginal utility*. It wouldn't just be less good, it would be *bad*:

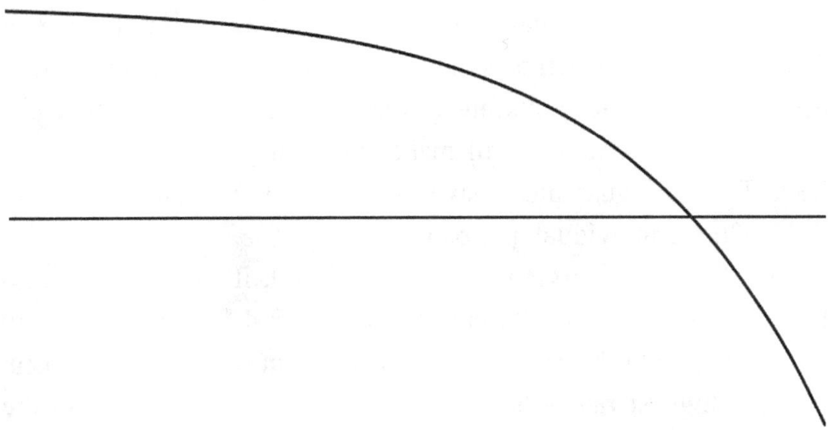

The concept of diminishing marginal utility builds on our understanding of needs. One reason we don't really need that much is because each additional unit of the same thing—jeans, headphones, horsepower—does less for us.

Diminishing marginal utility applies most obviously to spending. But it applies just as powerfully to other spheres of personal finance as well. Investing, for example.

Imagine a brand new industry that shows great promise. Startups launch, and eventually go public with much fanfare. In response, financial institutions create new actively managed funds chartered to buy stock in those companies.

Initially, the funds return well. But as more money flows into the funds, their managers are compelled to commit ever more capital to shares in the new ventures. That increases the prices of those shares. It's like a bidding war.

Eventually the stock prices reach such heights that the ventures' operating performance can't possibly fulfill the expectations behind them. Once earnings reports start making that clear, the stock prices drop, and the funds' returns fall.

Economists have a slightly different name for this: diminishing marginal *returns*. What fades here is quantifiable returns, not qualitative utility. But the idea is the same.

Diminishing marginal returns also applies to saving. In chapter 2 we saw how cash can be stored in high-yield online bank savings accounts. Those accounts are government insured. If a bank hits trouble, the government will make sure that you get your money back. But such guarantees have limits. The U.S. guarantees up to $250,000 per individual, per bank.[1]

So if you were trying to store $300,000; it would be wise to have accounts at two different banks. The first $250,000 could go to the bank with the highest interest rate. But often only one bank has that highest rate. The next best rate would be lower. So the remaining $50,000 would have to settle for less.

The laws of diminishing marginal utility and diminishing marginal returns don't always hold. Sometimes more really is required to deliver the desired result.

Consider headaches. If one aspirin doesn't work but two would, then the second aspirin would have more utility than did the first.

Or think again about savings accounts. As of this writing there are actually two online banks offering the same best interest rate. One could safely store up to half a million dollars in cash before having to settle for less.

But in general, the laws of diminishing marginal utility and diminishing marginal returns hold. Those on their way to wealth know this. They use these laws to moderate spending, skip hyped investment trends, and control their savings rate expectations.

SUMMARY

1. One more unit of a product tends to satisfy less than did the last.
2. One more investment in an asset tends to return less than did the last.

CHAPTER 7

INCENTIVES

Think

Odds	Fade
Risk	**Incentives**
Growth	
Needs	

People do what's in their interest. Me, for example.

When I teach, it's in my interest to get good evaluations from students at the end of a course. That boosts the odds that I'll have a popular class the next term, and supports the good reputation of the university. Plus, it's just plain satisfying. I want them. So if I can do something to earn good evaluations, I'm likely to do it.

Usually this works fine. The acts that draw good evaluations are generally the same acts that facilitate learning, which is my primary responsibility. But sometimes they're not.

Consider my value investing classes. Each week, I pick a public company for us to analyze. Over time, I've noticed that students tend to prefer companies that are in the headlines.

But sometimes a company in the news isn't great for driving home a key concept. It'll do, but it's not the best. And I may know of some other company—less storied, less dynamic—that would do a great job of driving home that concept.

But I skip it. I choose the one in the headlines.

Economists call this the *principal-agent problem*. An agent is someone hired by a principal to achieve some end. The problem arises when the agent is focused on one goal, and the principal is focused on a different goal. Agents' motivations keep them from fully delivering what the principals want.

I'm the agent, and the students are the principals. The students hired me to supply an outcome of learning. But I underperform.

Not by much, of course. In education, the disappointments caused by different incentives are usually minor. But in personal finance, they're major.

Take financial advisors. People hire them to manage their investments. I know many that are solid citizens. But their compensation packages can cause them to recommend financial products that stink.

For example, a friend of mine was recently encouraged by his financial advisor to take out a new mortgage on his home. The proposed mortgage was totally unnecessary, and deceptively expensive. No doubt the advisor would have received a commission from a lender for helping to originate new business.

That's legal. While American financial advisors are required to recommend *suitable* products, they're not required to be *fiduciaries*. They can suggest products that meet a client's needs, but they don't have to put their client's interests ahead of their own. So they don't.

Or consider real estate agents. They earn money on property transactions. An agent representing the seller of a home might personally earn about 1.5 percent of the final price. A $500,000 sale would therefore generate a $7,500 commission. But if no sale happens, the commission is zilch. Nada times 1.5 percent is nada. So the agent is motivated to just get sales *done*.

Imagine a home with a fair market value of $500,000. The owner engages an agent to sell it for full value. Imagine further that the agent gets a quick offer for $450,000, and recommends that the seller accept. That's $50,000 less than the seller had hoped for. But the agent's commission would still be $6,750. That may be $750 less than what the agent would have earned at the $500,000 price. But the agent might reason that the 10 incremental hours it would take to get that additional $750 isn't worth it. Better to apply those hours to selling a different property that doesn't yet have any bids.

I've been the principal in this kind of affair. Early in my career I was looking to lease a house in Annapolis, a nice sailing town near Washington DC. I didn't know the place well, and this was before the internet. So I engaged a real estate agent to help me. She knew what I wanted: a row house in the historic district. But she showed me apartments in an outlying 1980s development. I hated them. But that's what was in her inventory. I wound up having to find the row house on my own.

I had first heard about the principal-agent problem in an economics class at UCLA three years earlier. But it took Annapolis to really drive it home.

Real estate agents aren't evil. Neither are financial advisors. But their behavior is influenced by the incentive structures of their industries.

There's nothing intrinsically wrong with performance-based compensation. To the contrary, it's helpful. Without it, things might never get done. Imagine a real estate agent on a fixed salary tasked with selling a house. The agent wouldn't earn a commission for a successful transaction. So the sale would probably take longer to happen.

In short, performance-based compensation is a necessary part of commercial life. But it's imperfect. Exactly how imperfect is a matter of degree. There are good performance-based compensation plans, and bad performance-based compensation plans.

Good plans bring the agents' incentives closer to the principals' incentives. They can never be perfectly aligned, of course. But they can come close.

Bad plans are the opposite. They push the agents' incentives further away from those of the principals.

People on their way to wealth understand this. When they must work with professionals, they look for those motivated by good incentive compensation plans. That mitigates much of the damage that could otherwise come about, while increasing the odds that they'll get their desired result.

SUMMARY

1. Good compensation plans bring the agents' incentives closer to the principals' incentives.
2. Bad compensation plans push the agents' incentives away from the principals' incentives.
3. Incentives eclipse responsibilities.

CHAPTER 8

BIAS

Think

Odds	Fade
Risk	Incentives
Growth	**Bias**
Needs	

People think funny.

Not funny hilarious. Funny *wrong*. People misjudge.

We misjudge not because we're dumb. We misjudge because we're human. After all, we're not logic machines.

What's unfortunate is that we don't *realize* that we're not logic machines. We miss that we misjudge. And it's that failure that gets costly.

Consider my own misadventures with gold. One afternoon back in 1997 I was at the Newport Beach Public Library browsing through the investments section. I came across a book on gold, a subject of interest to me largely because I knew little about it. The first few pages read well, so I checked it out.

One of the book's more practical endorsements was of an outfit called the Rhode Island Hospital Trust. By some quirk of history, the trust owned a discount precious metals brokerage and storage vault. So I opened an account, and bought some gold bars at the then-prevailing price of $300 an ounce.

Precious metals don't pay interest like a bank account. Nor do they pay dividends like stocks. So I didn't earn anything while I owned the gold. Plus, the price languished at around $300 for years. Then one day in 2003 I got a call from the trust saying that they were getting out of the metals business. Would I like to sell my gold commission-free? Picturing an alternative of a payload of gold bars dumped on my driveway, I agreed to sell at $299 an ounce.

I didn't lose real money. But I certainly didn't make any.

Years later I would come to see that episode as riddled with my misjudgments. And I could have avoided them all had I recognized that, as a person, I was a blunder engine. Like everyone, I had *biases*.

Biases are flawed mental shortcuts. They cause misjudgments. They're also known as *cognitive biases* or *heuristics*. They're thinking tendencies that mislead.

They're particularly dangerous because they're hard to detect. It's not natural for us to notice our own biases. After all, they form innocently enough. They spring from our experiences. And experiences usually serve us well by helping us to form useful generalizations.

Consider weather. If after we see storm clouds it usually starts to rain, we may conclude that storm clouds lead to rain. That's a generalization. And it's a good one. We can use it to go indoors, or to fetch an umbrella, whenever we see storm clouds.

Now consider a different situation. Say that the first couple of times we saw storm clouds, our phone battery soon ran out of power. We might then generalize to see storm clouds as causing a dead phone. That would be wrong. And it could lead to funny behavior. Friends would wonder why every time the sky darkened we rushed for the nearest power socket.

In other words, experience sometimes misleads. It can cause us to generalize in ways that are incorrect. And when we do, we get biases.

I'm no psychologist. My formal training in psychology is limited to one introductory course at UCLA. But I've seen otherwise high-functioning people make bad money choices because of biases. Ten seem to be particularly perilous.

The first is *affinity*. It makes us want something because we like things tangentially associated with it. For example, we probably like the country that we live in. That could cause us to invest in bonds issued by our country. *Treasury bonds* in the U.S., for example. But the odds are that those will return less over time than would a low-cost stock index fund.

The affinity bias can also work backwards, keeping us from doing something constructive just because we dislike some inessential characteristic of it. For example, if the highest-yielding online bank savings account happens to come from a bank in a state we don't like, we might unproductively choose to stow money at a lower interest rate elsewhere.

The second bias is *anchoring*. It urges us to compare something to an insignificant baseline. For example, it can encourage us to sell a low-cost stock index fund just because its price soared past what we paid for it. In that case we'd be anchoring our decision on our cost. But that's the wrong baseline. What matters more is how well the index is likely to perform going forward.

Third is *authority*. It makes us follow leaders unthinkingly. If a prominent bank recommends a certain mutual fund, we may buy it even though its high fees make it unlikely to outperform a lower-cost alternative. Or if an established real estate agent advises us to accept a loss on the sale of a property during a down market, we may accept even though we have no pressing need to sell.

The authority bias can also work backwards, pushing us to reject good ideas because of where they come from. If an embarrassing uncle touts some high-yield bank savings account, we may reject it even though it really offers the highest available interest rate.

Fourth is *availability*. It has us making choices based on the facts that are most easily recalled, as opposed to the facts that are most pertinent. It has us focus on information that's more memorable than relevant. For example, if a neighbor recently made money on an angel investment, we may start angel investing despite that activity's low odds of success. Stated differently, the availability bias miscasts outliers as averages. It can fool us into misidentifying improbable events as normal.

Fifth is *consistency*. The consistency bias makes us favor actions that reaffirm our earlier actions. For example, if years ago we opened an account at a bank that later starts charging high fees, we may stay with that bank just because doing so seems to validate our earlier decision.

Note that consistency is different from *perseverance*. Perseverance is a virtue. It's sticking with a choice when any contrary indicators that emerge don't matter. For example, if we invest in a low-cost stock index fund and the price doesn't rise for months, it can be wise to hold fast. After all, those funds seem to perform well over the long term.

Consistency, by contrast, is sticking with a choice just because it was made. If a tax preparer we hired years ago starts filing our returns late, not finding someone new in the name of consistency would be silly.

Sixth is *confirmation*. It makes us favor ideas that support our preexisting views. It's like *consistency*, but without the need for *actions* as precedent. Mere *beliefs* suffice.

For example, if we always assumed that the best values in insurance came from the biggest carriers, but later found better values from specialized carriers, sticking with a big insurer would be wrong.

Seventh is *consensus*. It makes us do what's popular. It's a problem when we do something *just* because it's popular. An example would be if we bought some unnecessary insurance policy offered through work just because our colleagues were buying it.

Of course unpopularity doesn't guarantee success. Some ideas don't catch on for good reason. Few people invest in rare wines, and rightly so. It's a perennially underperforming type of asset.

Eighth is *reciprocity*. It makes us treat others as they have treated us. High-end retailers master this bias to advantage. For example, posh clothing store salespeople may graciously offer us imported sparkling water or espressos in the hopes that we'll reciprocate with a major purchase. That could make for a pretty expensive espresso.

Ninth is *selection*. It has us making decisions based on a set of facts that aren't representative. Consider peer-to-peer lending. It promises investors high rates of interest on loans made to other individuals through specialized online matching platforms.

In its early years, peer-to-peer lending looked attractive to some investors because the default rates were low. Borrowers paid interest and principal back, in full and on schedule. So the net returns were high. But as time went on the default rates soared. Net returns dwindled. Apparently the early days of the industry weren't representative. They were exceptional, not normal.

Like the availability bias, the selection bias makes outliers look like averages.

Tenth is *scarcity*. It makes us want things that seem to be in short supply. For example, we may offer too much for a house if we fear that the opportunity to own it may be lost to other bidders.

The scarcity bias can also disinterest us in things that seem to be available in abundance. Low-cost stock index funds, for example. They're easy to buy, and virtually costless to hold. It seems too simple. How could something so accessible return so well?

When we identify dangers, we can manage them. That's why understanding the 10 biases is so useful. Merely knowing how they can fool us keeps them from doing so. We can neutralize our misjudgments before they hurt us.

Biases are not a side issue. They're central. Many smart people blow money choices because they've never tackled their bad mental habits. There's even a field of study dedicated to the impact of psychology on economic decisions called *behavioral economics*.

Further, biases have become more dangerous. When I started managing my own money back in 1989, financial news generally came from a physical newspaper. To take action required putting down the newspaper, picking up the telephone, calling a bank or stockbroker, and giving instructions. That old-school flow had pauses during which haste could be halted. Reason had a chance to prevail.

But today, the internet has erased those pauses. It's now common for someone to scan the news in one app and trade in another. With smartphones, one needn't even stop walking. The nonstop stream denies prudence the opportunity to arrest blunders in the making. So understanding biases is more helpful now than ever.

Several biases can flare up at once. This can strengthen their harmful impact. Think again of my misadventure with gold. It was born of many biases ganging up to bamboozle me. The anchoring bias was at play, because in selling I focused on my cost, instead of on the more relevant future price of gold. The reciprocity bias was also in effect, as I was offered a commission-free sale. So too was the scarcity bias, since I knew that the commission-free opportunity would soon end.

That episode happened decades ago. But I'm just as vulnerable to biases as anyone else, and stand guard for the next outbreak.

People on their way to wealth know that they don't reason perfectly. They know that their logic isn't watertight. They accept that biases naturally cloud their judgment. So they don't let emotions or snap conclusions run their money. They're constructively skeptical about their intuitions. They muster the most objective mindset they can before making money choices.

SUMMARY

1. People naturally misjudge.
2. Most people don't recognize that they naturally misjudge.
3. People who accept that they naturally misjudge enjoy a rare advantage.
4. Misjudgments come from biases.
5. Smart people neutralize the threat of biases by decoupling instinct and action.

CHAPTER 9

DEPENDENCE

Think

Odds Fade
Risk Incentives
Growth Bias
Needs **Dependence**

Dependence is relying too much on something. It limits freedom. Smart people avoid it.

Dependence resembles addiction. We know that addiction is an increased need for nicotine, alcohol, or some other substance. Addiction is about chemicals.

But dependence—in the context of personal finance—is about sources of money or expertise.

Take work. People who depend on one employer for all of their money are vulnerable. It doesn't matter how healthy the employer seems, how long they've worked there, or how senior they are in the hierarchy. Things change. Industries shift, businesses merge, and economies falter. Downsizings, demotions, and reorganizations are common. People financially dependent on salaries who lose their job see their whole outlook darken.

Dependence on work doesn't just threaten employees. It threatens entrepreneurs, too. Consider a venture that makes most of its sales to one customer. If that customer cuts its budget, or starts paying invoices late, the entrepreneur suffers.

Same on the supply side. If the venture buys most of its materials from one supplier and no alternative vendor exists, an increase in the supplier's prices or a decrease in its responsiveness will hurt. That's why successful entrepreneurs strive for broad customer bases and broad supplier bases.

Smart people create for themselves a wide foundation of economic power. If they work for one company, they also have a portfolio of investments and cash that carries them through times that would otherwise be challenging. They're not scared of losing their job because they have financial assets to tide them over.

Stated differently, people on their way to wealth have sources of money that are *uncorrelated*. The sources act *separately*. If their job disappears, the price of their low-cost stock index fund doesn't automatically plunge, and their cash doesn't vanish. If the price of their low-cost stock index fund dips, they don't automatically get fired and their cash doesn't go away. Rot in one economic root doesn't cause rot in the others. One can never set these things up perfectly, of course. But one can come close.

Some people that work for a public company are encouraged—formally or informally—to buy its stock. Such an investment could be well intentioned. It could show faith in the corporation, and take advantage of an understanding of its industry.

But it would also increase dependence. It would create a correlation. If things go bad for the company, one could lose one's job at the same time that the company's stock price drops.

Of course smart people can still accept stock as part of their pay. Some employees get *restricted stock units* or *stock options* as a portion of their compensation.

Restricted stock units are shares that an employee receives over time. They're also called *RSUs*. Once received, an RSU can generally be sold for cash.

Stock options are similar. They give an employee the right to buy company shares at a predetermined price in the future, at which time they can be sold.

The worth of RSUs and stock options vary with the fortunes of the employer. But the employee doesn't pay cash up front for them. So getting them is different from buying shares on a stock exchange. That's why RSUs and stock options don't increase dependence in the way that outright stock purchases would.

Avoiding dependence is not the same thing as *diversification*. Diversification is allocating wealth among different assets or asset classes. But it can sometimes be silly, since some assets don't make sense to own. For example if someone has a job, cash, and holdings in a low-cost stock index fund, investing in fine art would constitute diversification. But fine art usually returns poorly. Investing in it is rarely intelligent. Avoiding dependence, by contrast, always is.

While dependence is often on sources of money, it can also be on sources of expertise.

Take financial advisors. If an advisor structures opaque tax shelters for a client, or puts the client in illiquid hedge funds run by distant managers, the client's ability to leave could be limited. Replacing the financial advisor could be difficult. The *switching costs* would be high.

Or consider bankers. In some countries it's prohibited to have mortgages with different banks on the same home. So some banks encourage homebuyers to take two mortgages, each with a different maturity date.

If when the shorter mortgage matures the homeowner replaces it with a new one, the homeowner may get stuck with a high rate of interest. That's because the banker knows that the longer original mortgage still in effect prevents the homeowner from borrowing at a lower rate from another bank. The staggered maturity dates of the two original mortgages made the client dependent on the banker.

Of course we want to work with financial advisors and bankers that we trust. People on their way to wealth get good at finding professionals that warrant their loyalty.

But trust does not require dependence. One can be loyal to competent experts without relying on them excessively.

Some dependencies are temporarily unavoidable. When new ventures launch, they may start with just one customer. When recent graduates take first jobs, they may rely on their salary. But smart people take steps to ensure that such dependencies are as short-lived as possible.

In some aspects of life dependence is a virtue. Marriage, for example. It pays to depend on your spouse. A couple with mutual dependency builds a sincere relationship of deserved trust. Anything else wouldn't work. The marriage would corrode if one spouse maintained the ability to switch in some misguided pursuit of independence.

But in personal finance, it's dependence that corrodes. Smart people see it as a threat. So from it they flee.

SUMMARY

1. Dependence is relying too much on a source of money or expertise.
2. People on their way to wealth have sources of money that are uncorrelated.
3. Trust does not require dependence.

PART II

SEE

CHAPTER 10

WORKING

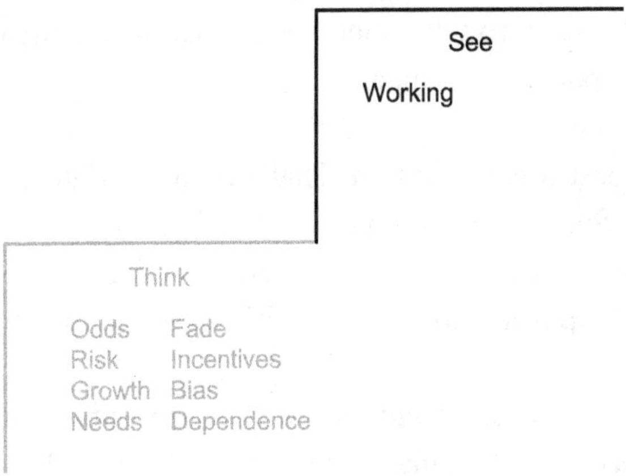

I need glasses. New students of mine get this in class one, much to their amusement. An unconscious act of mine tips them off.

I start my lectures bespectacled. Pacing to and fro, I gesticulate—towards the board, towards the students, towards the lectern—with energy. Then at some point my right hand floats up, grasps my glasses, and removes them. Now hinged to my thrashing hand, they flail like a conductor's baton.

Soon a thought, or a student's comment, draws my attention back to my notes on the lectern. But without glasses, my eyes can't adjust fast enough to the shorter distance. So my notes gaze back up at me, laughing, appearing to me like a blurred tray of salt and pepper.

I just got a new prescription, actually. The ophthalmologist used a phoropter—that's that bulky mask of lens wheels—to measure my sphere, cylinder, and axis. Those are the base factors that establish the parameters of the lenses. Once I get those lenses in new glasses, I can see clearly. Provided, of course, that I keep them on my face.

Personal finance also has base factors. We understand them now. They're the eight aspects of economic life: odds, risk, growth, needs, fade, incentives, bias, and dependence. With those established, we have lenses through which we can see with clarity the different spheres of personal finance.

Working, for example.

Working isn't the best way to get rich. That's because of taxes.

Income is taxed. Sometimes it's taxed at a high rate, and sometimes it's taxed at a low rate. The rate is determined in part by the total amount of a taxpayer's income. But it's also determined by the *type* of income.

Income from working is called *earned income.* It's subject to the *ordinary income tax rate*. And that's high. In 2021 it could get up to 37 percent at the federal level.[1]

To that is added state income tax. In California—the state more Americans live in than any other—it goes up to around 13 percent.[2]

So the total tax rate on earned income can reach about 50 percent.

Income from investing, by contrast, is often taxed at a lower rate. If an investment is sold after being held for over a year, the gain is taxed at up to 20 percent at the federal level. That was the top *long-term capital gains* tax rate in 2021.[3]

A *capital gain* is just the money you got from selling an asset, minus what you paid for that asset.

Adding in state tax—which for capital gains is often the same as for ordinary income—the total comes out to around 33 percent.

So with income from working, we get to keep half. With income from investing, we get to keep two-thirds. That's a big difference:

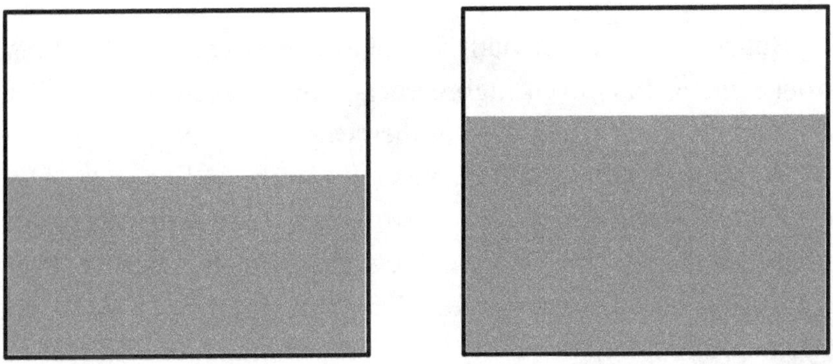

Each of the two black-bordered squares represents the same amount of pre-tax income. But the left square shows income from working. The right square shows income from investing. The gray areas are what, after taxes, we get to keep.

Casual thinking obscures this difference. When most folks see salaries, they see pre-tax salaries. When they see investment gains, they see pre-tax gains.

But that deceives. A $100,000 gross salary could yield the same amount after tax as a $75,000 investment gain. After all, half of $100,000 is $50,000; and so is two-thirds of $75,000.

There are many more wrinkles to income taxes than this simplistic presentation suggests. For example, certain kinds of investments trigger higher taxes. Other states have lower rates than California. And some earned income isn't taxed at all. But I've yet to see any jurisdiction where income from working is consistently taxed less than income from investing.

That's why smart people don't focus on pre-tax numbers. They focus on after-tax numbers. That lets them correctly view working as not their best source of wealth.

Of course some salaries are so gigantic that even at high ordinary income tax rates they cause wealth. Professional athletes, famous actors, and top executives get a lot of take-home pay regardless of how much they fork over to the government. Half of oodles is still oodles.

But such salaries are outliers, not averages. One shouldn't plan around them. Plus even high earners tend to keep more of their investment gains than they do of their earned income.

Working is still useful, of course. It's useful in five ways.

First, it's satisfying. Doing work you like with people you admire can be one of life's great rewards. No job is perfect; every profession has its drudgeries. But real joy can come from meaningful work, particularly since our communities rely on us to do the necessary tasks of society.

Second, it provides health insurance. Most working Americans have the bulk of their medical costs covered by their employer. Plus once someone has worked for a decade—once they or their spouse have had payroll taxes withheld for 40 quarters—they get healthcare inexpensively when they're older. Starting at age 65 they're qualified to get *Medicare part A*—basic government hospital insurance—at little cost.[4] More on that in chapter 22.

Third, work generates cash that can be used to pay for needs. Sure, it's taxed. But particularly early in our careers, earned income enables us to provide for ourselves and for those who depend on us.

Fourth, it facilitates savings. After-tax pay that isn't spent can be stockpiled in high-yield online bank savings accounts. As we'll soon see, that's a good way to kill worries.

Fifth, work accelerates investing. It does this most obviously by providing us with capital to invest, in the same way that it enables savings. But it accelerates investing in more powerful ways as well.

For one, work gives us the opportunity to set up advantaged accounts. They're advantaged in that they pay us bonuses.

Sometimes the bonus is a tax savings. The tax savings may come when we put money into the account, or when we take money out.

Other times the bonus is a subsidy. It's free money.

Take *401(k)s*. They're advantaged accounts that some companies offer to their employees. They provide a tax savings when money goes in. We contribute to them with part of our *gross* paycheck, before taxes are taken out. We put in *pre*-tax earnings.

Look back at the left side of the picture. When we contribute to a 401(k) we work with the big black-bordered box, not the smaller grey one. That is, not all of the white space goes to the government. Some of it stays with us.

Plus, many employers will match our contributions. Up to some limit, they'll throw in a percentage of what we put in. That's a subsidy. It's free money.

Employees of some public schools and nonprofit organizations may have access to an account similar to a 401(k) called a *403(b)*.[5] There's also a state and local government employee equivalent called a *457*.[6]

These plan names were not the brainchildren of branding wizards, obviously. They just refer to different sections of the tax code.

Other countries have plans similar to 401(k)s. Canada has a Registered Retirement Savings Plan, or RRSP; the UK has the self-invested personal pension, or SIPP; and Australia has Superannuation.

Another kind of advantaged account that work lets us establish is an *IRA*. It doesn't offer matching contributions, alas. But it does offer tax savings.

There are two main kinds of IRAs: traditional and Roth. A traditional IRA offers a tax savings when we put money in. It lets us make pre-tax contributions. It allows us to keep some of the white space.

Roth IRAs are different. They don't offer tax savings when money goes in. Only after-tax earned income can be contributed. But they do offer a tax savings when money comes out. In retirement, we can harvest the investment gains of a Roth IRA tax-free. All of the money is ours. When we withdraw from a traditional IRA, by contrast, we do pay tax.

Roth IRAs also have the advantage of never requiring withdrawals. We needn't ever take anything out. That means that wealth can keep growing tax-deferred inside of a Roth until we say so. That's unlike traditional IRAs. They have annual *required minimum distributions*. Since 2020 they start applying at age 72.[7]

A final advantage of Roth IRAs is that contributions to them can be withdrawn at any time without penalty. Returns earned on those contributions can't, but the contributions can. That provides some flexibility absent from traditional IRAs, which generally penalize withdrawals made before age 59½.[8]

Why the half? I have no idea.

IRAs aren't set up by employers. But it's still work that makes them possible. That's because contributions to them must come from earned income.

Most 401(k) plans are similar to a traditional IRA. They offer a tax savings when money goes in. For that reason they're sometimes called *traditional 401(k)s*. But there's also a version called a *Roth 401(k)*. It's more like a Roth IRA, offering a tax savings when money comes out.[9] They're less common, but some employers offer them.

There are plenty more nuances with 401(k)s, 403(b)s, 457s, traditional IRAs, and Roth IRAs. There are contribution limits, withdrawal conditions, and other terms. We'll touch on those later. But what's useful to note now is that the advantages they offer are enormous. And those advantages come to us only because of work.

Work accelerates investing mainly via advantaged accounts. But it also does so with RSUs (restricted stock units) and stock options. We saw those both back in chapter 9.

Not every employer chooses to offer RSUs or stock options. And some employers can't, because they have no stock. Governments and universities, for example. But because RSUs and stock options can only go to those who have jobs, they're properly viewed as another way that work facilitates investing.

It's easy to get fooled into thinking that work is the main way people get rich. For example, politicians promise to create new jobs as if that were the key to everyone's economic independence.

But that's not so. Work plays a role in a purposeful life, yes. But taxes clip its wealth-building potential. When it comes to building real financial autonomy, a job is just the start.

SUMMARY

1. Smart people focus on after-tax numbers, not pre-tax numbers.
2. Income from working is generally taxed at a higher rate than income from investing.
3. Working therefore contributes less to wealth than does investing.
4. Working is nonetheless useful because it's satisfying, often provides health insurance, pays for needs, facilitates saving, and accelerates investing.

CHAPTER 11

SPENDING

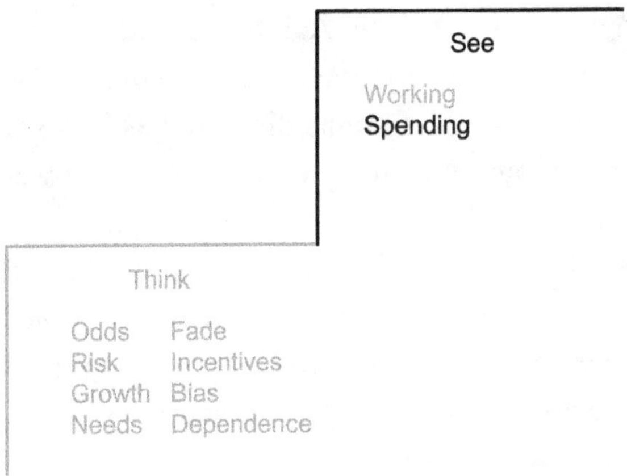

Spending is swapping money for products to consume.

Products include both goods, which are tangible; and services, which are intangible.

Done well, spending serves needs. Done poorly, it's enslaved to wants.

Spending done well is *deliberate*. It's done *consciously*. It has three hallmarks: pauses, bids, and budgets.

First are pauses. Those are healthy waiting periods that smart people impose on themselves before buying anything. They're intentional delays. They can be based on money, or they can be based on products.

Some pauses are based on money. People on their way to wealth may have a policy of hanging on to any cash they earn for a while before using it. They just keep it in the bank for a period. That period may be a day, a week, or a month. They get to pick how long it is. But only after that period do they allow themselves to spend it.

Other pauses are based on products. Some smart people have a rule requiring them to wait before making any contemplated buy. When an urge to purchase something wells up, they delay. That delay could be for a day, a week, a month. Again, they choose.

Both kinds of pauses are constructive. They're constructive because they provide enough time for wants disguised as needs to be unmasked. They strip impulses of their wealth-eroding power. They allow passing fancies to fade away, forever unmissed.

Aggressive salespeople can make the merit of a pause hard to appreciate. That's because they take advantage of the *scarcity bias*. They may claim that the chance to buy something is short-lived, citing low levels of inventory or upcoming price increases. *We're running out. The discount ends tonight.*

Ads are similar. They can leverage the *affinity bias*. They're crafty at attaching love, or power, or attractiveness to a product in a sneaky attempt to get us to buy.

Same with famous personalities. They awaken in us the *authority bias*. Celebrities and influencers are respected, motivating some to purchase goods and services that they endorse.

But smart people aren't fooled. They know about the scarcity, affinity, and authority biases. They see right through little stunts.

Pauses aren't perfect. They don't guarantee intelligent spending. One could want something expensive and unnecessary, buy it after a week, and it will still be expensive and unnecessary. But on balance pauses decrease the odds of such squandering.

The second hallmark of spending done well is bids. It's getting quotes for the same product from different vendors. It's an idea that comes from corporations. Well-run firms have a policy of getting three bids before buying anything big.

The three-bids rule is obviously useful for uncovering the least expensive way to fulfill a need. But it can be helpful in other ways as well.

For example, I once needed a new patio umbrella for my Northern California house. Patio umbrellas are often sold as complete sets. But in gathering three bids I learned that they have two separate components: the umbrella itself, consisting of the pole and the canopy; and the base, the heavy bottom that holds the pole upright.

This was a useful finding because the bases that come with most complete sets are too lightweight. They're not sturdy enough. They let a strong wind topple the umbrella with ease. If that happens when friends are gathered on the deck, someone could get skewered by the tip of one of the canopy-supporting ribs.

The heaviest bases, it turns out, are sold separately. They're made of poured concrete. They're so heavy that only hurricanes have a chance against them. So I paired one from a home improvement store with a high quality wood-and-canvas umbrella from a different retailer. The setup served handsomely for over a decade. Plus, no cookout guests got harpooned.

In that case the three-bids rule didn't lead me to the least expensive option. It led me to the most expensive option, actually. But it was the highest *quality* option, which probably turned out to have the lowest cost *per year*.

The three-bids rule has limits. For example, it would be silly to use it for tiny purchases. Those can be done quickly, without peril. But for any buy of size, it increases the odds of acting intelligently.

The third hallmark of spending done well is budgets. Budgets can be formal, or informal. Formal budgets are made with spreadsheets, or online tools. Informal ones are just a basic awareness of how much one should spend. Both can work.

Formal or informal, budgeting takes two forms: *income-based* and *zero-based.*

Income-based budgeting caps purchases at *take-home pay.* It vetoes buys in excess of after-tax earned income. It stops us from spending more than we make.

Zero-based budgeting imposes a different kind of limit. It requires each expense to justify itself. It's another idea from corporations.

If one spent some amount on clothes last month, that has no bearing on how much one should spend on clothes this month. Precedent doesn't matter. One must truly need the clothes. The default assumption is that the appropriate amount to spend is zero.

Of course people are not companies. It could be overkill for everyone to adopt some corporate procurement model. But zero-based budgeting has real merit. It reminds smart people that they're allowed to require something they buy to *work for them.* It's an *employee.*

The most useful budgets are income-based *and* zero-based. They're both. They allow only those purchases that fit under a take-home pay cap, and that are necessary. This dual-rule approach has great advantages.

For one, it doesn't allow an increasing income to automatically drive up spending. After all, there's no requirement that one has to buy more goods and services just because one can.

Many people miss this. As their income rises, they spend more. They get locked into an ever-escalating consumption competition. Those competitions are endless. Endless, and unwinnable.

Another advantage to the dual-rule approach is that it keeps budgeting from becoming a threat. Budgeting is a plan to spend. But as we'll see, planning *not* to spend is a better way to build wealth. Zero-based budgeting, matched with a hard spending limit centered on income, makes *not spending* more doable.

Spending done poorly also has hallmarks. There are three: haste, facade, and debt.

First is haste. It's spending without pause. It's common. Most people don't constructively delay. Instead, they rush. They're putty in the hands of salespeople leveraging the scarcity bias, advertisers wielding the affinity bias, and influencers brandishing the authority bias.

Second is facade. Some folks see bold spending as wealth itself. They're fooled by the disguise. But that kind of spending just masquerades as abundance. It doesn't prove any ability to buy. Instead, it proves an enslavement to wants.

Third is debt. In most cases, borrowing money to spend reveals a purchase best postponed. There may be exceptions, as we'll see. But a deferrable buy made with a loan is usually a buy that should never have happened.

Unnecessary spending is costlier than it first appears. Consider a product with a $1,000 price tag. Initially, $1,000 might seem to be the extent of the damage. But if the product wasn't purchased, that $1,000 could be invested. In a low-cost stock index fund, that might yield 7 percent after tax per year on average. After 30 years, that would turn the $1,000 into over $8,000.

It gets worse if the product was bought with borrowed money. We've seen how credit cards in the U.S. charge an average of about 15 percent per year on outstanding balances.[1] So if the purchase was made with a credit card and the balance wasn't paid off for four years, over $800 in interest would be charged. Added to the initial product price and foregone investment gains, the total cost of the item would exceed $8,800.

That's almost *nine times* the original price tag.

Admittedly, this is a simplified view. It relies on the product being truly unneeded. The investment gain wouldn't happen for decades. And credit card debt is among the most expensive kind of borrowing that there is.

But the point is solid. Unnecessary things cost a lot. They cost their price, plus foregone investment returns, plus any interest on money borrowed to buy them.

That's why smart people spend selectively. They're on their way to wealth in part *because* they spend selectively.

Spending and investing are different. While spending is buying products to consume, investing is committing capital in pursuit of a return. Seeing this difference yields a useful view on homes.

The purchase of a home is best viewed as spending. That's because its main purpose is to have a place to live. The real product—housing—is consumed.

Many aspects of a home make it look like an investment. It lasts a long time. Its market price is generally included in your net worth calculation. And if you sell the home, you may realize a gain.

Plus if you've lived in the home for at least two of the last five years, that gain may be tax free up to a limit. Since 1997 the limit has been $250,000, or $500,000 for a married couple that files a joint tax return.[2] That's a lot.

But as we'll see later, the returns from home sales often just match the rate of inflation. There's commonly no gain in *real* terms.

Of course some people do better. Some make a career out of buying and selling real estate. But that's a job, not a sideline. Plus, they usually rely on *leverage*. They borrow most of the money needed to buy a property, putting in little of their own cash.

When leverage works, it works fantastically. It works fantastically because any gain is measured against not the total purchase price of a property, but just the portion that was paid with one's own money.

But when leverage doesn't work, it's a disaster. That's because if one realizes a loss, one still has to pay back the lender. If there was no gain, that may be challenging.

Seeing a home purchase as spending reduces the odds of that disaster. It properly puts the focus on our need for housing. It helps to prevent overpaying. We're willing to pony up a fair price for a place to live. But we're not thrilled to pay too much for an investment that's likely to underperform.

Borrowing money to buy something creates an interest cost. That's bad. But at least you own the something.

What would be nuts, of course, is borrowing to *not* own the something. No one would take on debt just to have the *use* of the something, without ever owning it. Or would they?

You bet they would. They do it all the time. It's called *leasing*.

Leasing is common with cars. Its appeal is that the monthly payments are generally lower than they would be if the car was bought with an auto loan.

It may not be intuitive to view leasing as borrowing. But it is. There are two ways to see this.

First, a lease is an obligation every bit as real as a loan from a bank. Its required monthly payments make it a debt in everything but name.

Second, the *lessor*—the outfit that owns the car—has itself borrowed money to buy the car. So it has an interest cost. It passes that cost along to the *lessee*—the consumer—by burying it in the monthly payments. So the lessee effectively reimburses the lessor for interest. Economically, that's indistinguishable from the lessee paying the interest directly.

Leasing has other problems as well. For example, the lessee may be responsible for maintenance costs. Different leases have different conditions, of course. But it's not unusual for the driver to have to pay for repairs and upkeep. And yet at the end of the lease period the lessee owns nothing. They can't sell the car, because it's not theirs.

In fairness, there are occasions when leasing may make sense. Take someone who accepts a one-year work assignment out of state. That person will need a place to live for a predefined period of time. So it may be best for them to lease a home. That would spare them the trouble of having to start and end the year with a real estate transaction.

Or consider a situation where someone lives in a high-cost area. In America's big coastal cities it can actually make more sense to lease a home than to buy it. More on that in chapter 18.

But outside of some particular circumstances, leasing is deceptively expensive.

It's initially hard to see just how careful most rich people are with spending. After all, some rich people spend lavishly. Most, it sometimes seems.

But big-spending rich people are more visible than smart-spending rich people. After all, it's the big-spending rich people that flash themselves around and catch our attention. So that's the behavior that we notice. The availability bias urges us to see it as average.

But it's not average. It's outlying. Most rich people don't regard lavish spending as the purpose of their wealth. Instead, they see smart spending as one of its causes.

SUMMARY

1. Spending is swapping money for products to consume.
2. Done well, spending serves needs.
3. Done poorly, spending is enslaved to wants.
4. Good spending is marked by pauses, bids, and budgets.
5. Bad spending is marked by haste, facade, and debt.
6. The best budgets are both income-based and zero-based.
7. Unnecessary spending is deceptively expensive because of foregone investment returns and interest expense.
8. Spending and investing are different.
9. Leasing is useful only in specific circumstances.

CHAPTER 12

BORROWING

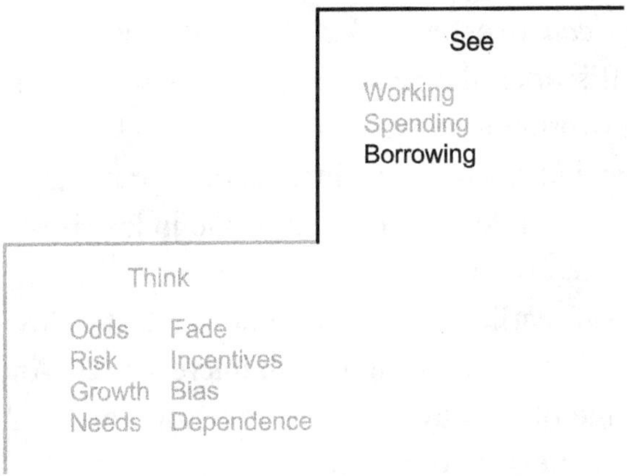

Borrowing increases risk.

It doesn't always cause catastrophes, of course. It doesn't guarantee big losses. Under some circumstances it can even be useful. For example, early in a career borrowing can let one meet needs that might otherwise go unfulfilled.

But in general, borrowing money is best viewed as increasing risk. It increases risk by adding expenses that boost the chance of loss.

Borrowing requires repayment, costs money, or both.

The amount that must be repaid is called the *principal*, *balance*, or *outstanding amount*. The process of paying down principal is called *amortization*.

I don't mean to throw a dictionary at you here. But some day some lending officer is going to say *principal*, or *balance*, or try to draw some nonexistent distinction between the two, and you'll feel better having a solid grip on the terms.

The costs of a borrowing can be *fees* or *interest*. A fee is a set amount, like $20. Interest, by contrast, is a percentage.

Interest can be *fixed* or *floating*. Fixed means the percentage doesn't change.

Floating means the percentage can change. A floating interest rate is set at some *spread* over an *index*. The index is a base, variable interest rate. It's often the *prime rate*. That's what banks charge their most creditworthy borrowers.

To illustrate, if the index is 1 percent and the spread is 10 percent, the floating interest rate is 11 percent. If the index rises to 2 percent, the floating interest rate rises to 12 percent.

Index is a term we saw earlier. We saw it in the context of low-cost stock index funds. Now we're using it with interest rates. And later we'll use it in some other ways. What's common among all the uses is that it always refers to some benchmark or standard.

Borrowing takes many forms. One is *loans*. Loans can be from a bank or other financial institution, or from a person.

A loan can be *unsecured*, meaning not *collateralized* by anything. In that case the lender can't take anything away from the borrower if the debt isn't repaid.

Or, a loan can be *secured*. That means it's collateralized. A car loan is secured by a car. A *mortgage* is secured by a home.

A second form borrowing can take is *credit card debt*. Charges to a credit card that are not paid off on time generally incur both interest and fees.

Third is a *line of credit*. It's a standing opportunity to borrow money up to some limit from a bank or other financial institution.

It's *revolving*, meaning that it can be repeatedly drawn from and paid back.

Like loans, lines of credit can be secured or unsecured. An example of a secured line of credit is a *HELOC*, or *home equity line of credit*. It's collateralized by a home that already has a mortgage on it. That makes it a *second mortgage*.

An example of an unsecured line of credit is a credit card.

A fourth form of borrowing is *overdue bills*. Amounts past due to cable companies, utilities, and other vendors often incur interest charges and late fees.

Fifth is *overdrafts*. They're withdrawals from a bank account in excess of the amount in that account. The bank automatically lends enough money to cover the deficit in exchange for a fee.

Sixth is *margin accounts*. They're offered by securities brokerages. They let one borrow money from the brokerage to make investments through that brokerage. One's own capital in the margin account collateralizes the borrowing.

Sometimes borrowing increases risk a lot. That makes it *threatening debt*. Other times it increases risk only a little. It's *not-so-threatening debt*. Fortunately, it's easy to see in advance which is which. Take threatening debt. Four warning signs flag it.

First, it's expensive. It has a high rate of interest, high fees, or both. If it has a high *floating* rate of interest, that's probably because it has a big spread.

Second, it's used to buy unneeded things. It finances the purchase of mere wants.

Third, it's used to buy something likely to fall in value. Most things wear out. Boats, shoes, and other goods usually drop in worth every year. They *depreciate*.

Fourth, it has no tax benefits. Interest paid on it isn't *tax deductible*, unlike some other kinds of debt that we'll see.

An example of threatening debt is a *subprime* auto loan on a luxury vehicle. It's threatening in all four ways.

First, it has a high rate of interest. Subprime means that the borrower isn't considered very creditworthy. So a lender will charge more in exchange for assuming a higher risk of default.

Second, a luxury vehicle isn't *needed* in the way that a more standard car might be.

Third, cars depreciate. Parts age, paint fades, and brake pads wear thin.

Fourth, auto loans don't offer tax benefits. I've yet to see a government that encourages personal vehicle ownership by making interest paid on car loans tax deductible.

While debt with all four warning signs is certainly threatening, debt with just one, two, or three can be plenty threatening as well. It's a matter of degree.

Not-so-threatening debt looks better. It has the opposite four hallmarks.

First, it's inexpensive. It has a low rate of interest, and low or no fees. If the interest rate floats, the spread is small and is based on a standard index like the prime rate.

Second, it's used to satisfy a need. Products bought with it are necessities.

Third, it's used to buy something likely to rise in value. It finances the purchase of products that *appreciate*.

Fourth, it offers a tax benefit.

An example of not-so-threatening debt is a *conforming* mortgage on a home. It has all four characteristics. First, it has an interest rate that's lower than that of other mortgages. That's because it's conforming, which basically means that it's below a certain threshold. In 2021 that threshold was usually $548,250. In so-called high cost areas it got up to $822,375:[1]

http://www.smallstepstorich.com/12.1.htm

Nonconforming mortgages cost more. The most common kind of nonconforming mortgage is a *jumbo* mortgage. Jumbo means it's over the threshold.

Mortgages can be nonconforming for other reasons as well. For example, it could be nonconforming if the borrower has a high *debt-to-income ratio*. That generally means that the borrower's monthly debt payments divided by monthly gross income is above 43 percent.[2]

Second, one needs a place to live. The home bought with it can be viewed as a necessity.

Third, homes tend to appreciate. They may appreciate only at the rate of inflation, as we've seen. Plus the faucets, flooring, and other components *de*preciate. But prices of homes still tend to rise because a growing population makes the space they occupy and the right to inhabit them worth more.

Fourth, they offer a tax benefit. Interest paid on a primary residence mortgage is generally tax deductible. That means you can subtract it from income for the purposes of calculating how much federal income tax you owe. That's good.

Most homeowners can deduct all of their mortgage interest payments. But some bump up against limits. The limits are based on the size of the mortgage. Currently, interest paid on only the first $750,000 of a mortgage is deductible. The limit rises to $1,000,000 if the mortgage was taken out before December 16, 2017.[3]

So my apologies if you happen to have bought your mansion on the 17th.

While borrowings that increase risk only a little are *not-so-threatening*, they're not exactly *good*. That's because unless it has a negative interest rate—unless some freak lender pays you to take it—borrowing is never intrinsically advantageous. No sensible person takes on an obligation for its own sake. Instead they choose the freedom from debt that marks economic independence.

It's easy to see how borrowing increases risk. It increases risk because it adds expenses that lead to losses.

For example, in chapter 11 we imagined the purchase of a product with a $1,000 price tag. We saw how if it was bought with a credit card that charged 15 percent on the outstanding balance and the amount wasn't paid back for four years, the interest expense would be over $800. That is, over $800 would be lost.

One reason that loss is big is because of what that 15 percent actually means. A credit card statement showing an interest rate of 15 percent is showing the *annual percentage rate*, or *APR*. Credit card companies have to disclose it.

But APR underestimates real cost. That's because it doesn't capture the effect of compounding within a year. How cruel that compounding is depends on how often the credit card company calculates interest charges.

Many do so *daily*. That's bad. Every 24 hours they multiply the balance by the APR, then divide the result by 365. So each day the balance grows because it includes an interest charge. That nasty antic is called the *daily balance method*.

After a month of the daily balance method, the original $1,000 outstanding amount would have triggered interest charges of around $12. After a year, $162. And after four years, $822.

Those charges are a result of the *annual percentage yield*, or *APY*. It's higher than the APR. That's because it *does* capture the effect of compounding within a year. It's the rate that matters. But credit card companies are allowed to keep it under wraps.

With the daily balance method, an APR of 15 percent would translate into an APY of just over 16 percent. That makes a difference. In our example it means extra interest charges of $73.

Another example of how borrowing increases risk is with margin accounts. We saw how they let one borrow money from a financial institution to make investments.

As we've seen, a low-cost stock index fund is likely to return 7 percent per year after tax. If one invested $1,000 in such a fund and the first year was average, the return would be $70.

Now picture borrowing $500 from the financial institution at 6 percent interest. In the first year the interest cost would be $30.

The borrowing would let one invest a total of $1,500. That amount times 7 percent equals $105. And that number minus the interest expense of $30 equals $75. So with the borrowing, the return goes up to $75.

Since $75 is more than $70, borrowing would seem to increase returns. But there are two problems with that: collateral and volatility. They act in tandem to slay clients.

First, collateral. Financial institutions require a client's own holdings to equal at least some multiple of the amount borrowed. That multiple might be two, for example. In that case a client that borrowed $500 would have to make sure to always have at least $1,000 of their own in the account. The $1,000 would secure the $500 borrowing. That becomes an issue due to the second problem: volatility. A fund may return 7 percent per year on average. But it doesn't do so smoothly. It does so bumpily.

Picture the total investment starting its first day at $1,500. Stock prices tend to go up, so perhaps the next day it rises to $1,502. The next day, $1,505. So far, so good.

But maybe the following week the market dips, as it commonly does. That might cause the investment to temporarily drop to, say, $1,200. The $500 loan is still outstanding, so only $700 in the account belongs to the client. That's just $1,200 minus $500. That would put the client in violation of the collateral rule. It would drag the multiple below two, to 1.4. That's just $700 divided by $500. And that's bad.

In such a case the financial institution may make a *margin call.* It may compel the client to sell part of the fund to have adequate cash to pay back enough of the loan to bring the multiple back up to two. Here, $150 would suffice. That would bring the loan down to $350. And $700 divided by $350 is two.

The problem is that that sale would have been forced at a moment when stock prices were down. It would make the client sell below cost. That's a loss. And that loss would have come directly from the risk created by borrowing.

Debt is tempting. It promises to let us consume more, and to juice our investment returns. But it boosts risk. It invites loss. That's an invitation that smart people don't willingly extend.

SUMMARY

1. Borrowing increases risk.
2. Borrowing requires repayment, costs money, or both.
3. Debt is threatening if it increases risk a lot.
4. Threatening debt is high cost, is used to buy unneeded products that depreciate, and lacks tax advantages.
5. Debt is not-so-threatening if it increases risk only a little.
6. Not-so-threatening debt is low cost, is used to buy needed products that don't depreciate, and offers tax advantages.

CHAPTER 13

SAVING

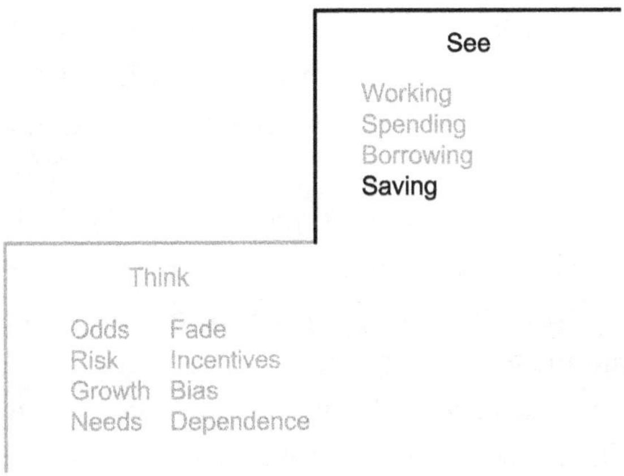

Saving is stockpiling earned cash.

It's useful because it erases worry. It eliminates the concern that one won't have enough money to pay for needs. Some needs are anticipated; some are surprises. But savers don't care. They're ready for either.

Saving also sets the stage for investing. As we've seen, investing offers real returns. But to do it, one needs cash. Savers have it.

Savings have to be housed somewhere. A bank checking account, for example. That's one where earned income lands, and from which bills are paid. It works fine. Plus, it's insured. We've seen how in the U.S. the Federal Deposit Insurance Corporation backs accounts for up to $250,000 per individual, per bank.[1] Other countries have FDIC equivalents, like the CDIC in Canada and the FSCS in the UK.

But checking accounts aren't great. They often charge a monthly fee, and don't pay interest.

An alternative is a *cash management account* at a major discount brokerage. It's also called a *CMA*. It can be used to receive salaries and pay bills, just like a checking account. But it generally doesn't charge monthly fees, and does pay interest.

Plus even though it's not from a bank, a CMA is probably still government insured. That's because the brokerage *sweeps* CMA balances into real banks whose FDIC insurance passes through to the CMA account holder.

Another alternative is a *money market account*, or *MMA*. It's FDIC-insured like a CMA,[2] and can also be used to receive salaries and pay bills. But it doesn't sweep balances into banks. Instead, it puts them into the *money market*.

The money market is simple to understand. Remember *bonds*? That term is actually finance shorthand for *fixed income securities*. They're borrowings by governments and companies that promise to pay interest, and to repay principal.

The money market is part of the fixed income securities market. It's the part that's least likely to default. It includes *Treasurys* and *commercial paper*.

Treasurys—oddly yet correctly spelled—are issued by the U.S. government. They're unlikely to default because the U.S. is particularly creditworthy. Plus it's the proud owner of a printing press that could—in a pinch—be fired up to spit out new dollars to pay whatever it owes. Your interest and principal, for example.

Commercial paper is short-term borrowings by established corporations. It's unlikely to default because it's issued by solid firms, and because it quickly *matures*. That's when the borrowing has to be paid back. Commercial paper generally matures nine months after it's issued. That's not much time for an established corporation to fail.

A drawback to MMAs is that only the first six transactions per month are free. But an MMA might still make sense if it offers interest rates much higher than CMAs.

Checking accounts, CMAs, and MMAs can all store money. But they're designed to facilitate inflows and outflows of cash, not to impress you with high interest rates. So as your cash piles up, it's smart to also open a savings account. It pays more interest. Savings accounts are offered by banks, including those that offer checking accounts.

But better ones can come from banks whose presence is primarily online. They offer high-yield online savings accounts. The best ones are easy to find on comparison websites:

http://www.smallstepstorich.com/13.1.htm

A good high-yield online savings account has five characteristics.

First, it offers a high rate of interest. The rate will float, which means that it can float down. But banks that attract deposits with high rates tend to maintain high rates. They know that if they don't, you'll leave.

The interest rate that online savings banks tout is usually the *annual percentage yield*, or *APY*. Unlike the APR (annual percentage rate), the APY captures the effect of compounding within a year. It's higher. No wonder they tout it.

Like credit card companies, banks usually compound interest daily. But with savings, that's good. That's because now interest is what you're getting, not what you're paying.

Second, the account is easy to use. It's simple to open, and has a straightforward website. If you call the online bank on the phone, they answer.

Third, it's government insured. If the bank fails, the FDIC will step in and back your deposits.

Exceeding the insured limit at a single bank would be foolish. It would increase risk, for nothing. Fortunately, it's not necessary. That's because many different online banks offer attractive rates. One could open accounts at several.

Fourth, the account is free. It doesn't charge for deposits and withdrawals, nor for opening or closing the account.

Fifth, it's denominated in the currency of your expenses. That generally means that it's located in your country of residence.

Saving in a different currency isn't really saving. It's investing. And since cash—domestic or foreign—usually offers meek returns, it's *bad* investing.

People that spend time in different countries routinely scuffle with an *exchange rate*. That's the price of one currency expressed in terms of another.

Most exchange rates float. They change over time. Others are *pegged*, or fixed. But whether floating or pegged, the exchange rate for a given currency pair comes in three flavors.

First is the *buying rate*. It's the amount of one currency that a buyer will pay for a different currency. Such a buyer could be a bank, or a currency exchange counter of the sort one sees in airports.

Second is the *selling rate*. It's the opposite. It's the amount of one currency that a seller—again, like a bank or foreign exchange counter—will pay for a different currency. Unsurprisingly, it's higher than the buying rate.

Third is the *mid-market rate*. It's the midpoint between the buying rate and the selling rate. It's the number that a news article might quote. And it's the one that respectable exchange services tend to advertise.

Some characteristics of online accounts don't matter. For instance, it's unimportant what part of the country the bank is located in. My base in America is California. But I have an account at a bank in New York, a state I haven't been to for decades. That's caused no difficulties.

It also doesn't matter that an online account doesn't come with checkwriting, ATM cards, or other standard features. It doesn't matter because one links it to a checking account, CMA, or MMA that does.

Online accounts make sense to use even when interest rates are low. It makes sense for two reasons.

First, even a slightly higher rate makes a difference as one's savings grow. The amount of interest received really does get bigger. An extra 1 percent times a significant number equals a significant extra.

Second, it encourages the good habit of seeking out the best returns available for a given asset class. One who wins with cash tends to win with stocks.

A different sort of institution where one could save is a *credit union*. Deposits there are backed by the *NCUA*, or *National Credit Union Administration*. Like the FDIC with banks, the NCUA backs accounts for up to $250,000 per individual, per credit union.[3]

Some credit unions offer high interest rates. They tempt. But those rates often apply only to savings up to some modest level, like $1,000. Amounts over that earn much less.

There's nothing wrong with receiving salaries and paying bills with a credit union account. It can even feel clubby, since different credit unions serve different groups. There's the Actors Federal Credit Union for actors,[4] the SchoolsFirst Federal Credit Union for teachers,[5] and the Lee Federal Credit Union for—I am not making this up—folks with the last name Lee.[6] I actually know someone who qualifies for all three. But providing a high-yield home for cash seems not to be a credit union strength.

Financial institutions—online and otherwise—offer ways to stockpile cash besides high-yield online savings accounts. Some may seem attractive, since they sport higher rates. But they can also increase risk.

Certificates of deposit, for example. They're also called *CDs* or *time deposits*. They lock up cash for a period like six months or a year. They feature fixed rates of interest that are usually above the floating rate offered by the same institution. If the cash is withdrawn prematurely, a penalty is applied that can easily wipe out the bonus interest.

Theoretically, one could take advantage of the higher rates by allocating just a portion of savings to a CD. But that portion would have to be limited to that which definitely wouldn't be needed during the lockup period. Any more would increase risk. It would do so by inviting an early withdrawal penalty.

Another alternative is *fixed income funds*. Many vow to act like cash. They channel money into securities unlikely to default, like Treasurys and commercial paper. In fact a fund with those very assets would be called a *money market fund*. It's different from a money market *account* in that its price can fluctuate like—but probably less than—a listed stock.

The rate offered by money market funds is often presented as a *7-day yield*. That's whatever the fund earned over the last seven days, *annualized*. It's scaled up to approximate what it would pay out over a year.

A money market fund's 7-day yield is comparable to a savings account's APR. That's because it doesn't capture the effect of compounding. The 7-day *effective* yield, however, does. Sometimes that's the figure given to describe the performance of a money market fund. It's also referred to as simply the *effective yield* or the *compound yield*. It's comparable to a savings account's APY.

Some fixed income funds venture beyond Treasurys and commercial paper into higher-yielding securities that money market funds wouldn't touch. Corporate bonds, for example. They have longer original times to maturity than commercial paper. That gives them more time to default.

That doesn't mean that they will, of course. In fact fixed income funds that present themselves as safe havens generally stick to securities that are *investment grade*. That means that their interest and principal are reasonably expected to be paid as promised.

The problem with such fixed income funds is the same as the problem with money market funds: volatility. The price fluctuates. The amount you put in might not always be fully available to take out.

Back in chapter 3 we saw how volatility isn't the same thing as risk. We illustrated that with listed stocks. In long-term investing, the inevitable short-term blips in stock prices aren't scary. They're normal.

But in saving, volatility matters. We don't want blips in the price of our saved cash. We want it to always be there. That's how fixed income funds can come up short.

Another problem with fixed income funds is that sometimes—rarely, but sometimes—they freeze up. This happened in March 2020, for example. As the severity of the coronavirus pandemic became clear, a few bond funds briefly blocked withdrawals.[7] That may have caused some people to pay bills late, triggering fees and interest charges.

There's a simple test to see if an account is safe for savings. Just ask, is the account able—promptly, fully, and always—to pay for needs without penalty?

Some savers choose not to earn interest because their religion prohibits it. They're well served by accounts that are both FDIC-insured and free of fees. Financial institutions offer plenty of such options.

It's tempting not to save. We know that sharp sales professionals, seductive ads, and celebrity spokespeople activate the biases that urge us to spend instead.

Fortunately, there's a simple way to crush temptation: automatic savings plans. One can have a set amount of earned income periodically stowed away as savings. Pay from work is direct deposited to a checking account, CMA, or MMA; and then part of it is automatically forwarded to an online savings account. Such a setup can cast in stone a healthy habit.

Even though saving erases worry and facilitates investing, it's not perfect. The big problem is inflation. As we know, the odds are that prices will go up. Time erodes the purchasing power of stockpiled cash.

Unfortunately, interest doesn't solve this problem. That's because it's taxed. And the rate at which it's taxed is often the same high rate that's applied to salaries and wages. So even if the gross interest paid by an online bank keeps pace with inflation, the after-tax interest doesn't.

That's one reason why it's possible to save too much. One can *oversave*. Oversaving happens when it's *underinvesting*. It happens when staying in cash blocks one from the higher returns that come from a more promising asset class.

Happily, it's easy to identify the point at which saving drifts into underinvesting. It happens when savings fly past a reasonable multiple of one's expenses.

I know about how much I spend each year. I like to keep about three years' worth of that amount in high-yield online savings accounts. That's my multiple: three.

That's probably higher than necessary. But for my peace of mind, it makes sense. When I know that I can shoulder three years' worth of my family's costs regardless of what happens in the stock market or the economy, I'm calm. That to me is luxury.

The right multiple varies by the person. Generally, it grows as one gets older. A 20 year old just finishing college might reasonably aspire to saving a quarter of a year's worth of expenses. A retiree approaching 80, maybe several years' worth.

Of course momentary spikes in savings can be acceptable. The normal cash buffer is annual expenses times some multiple. But a hoard above that could make sense in anticipation of a major purchase. For example if one were about to make a down payment on a home, savings could reasonably expand to equal the buffer plus the down payment.

That could even make tools besides high-yield online savings accounts useful. Assume you were certain that you were going to make a down payment on a home in exactly one year. Assume further that the rate offered on a one year FDIC-insured CD was much higher than that offered by the best high-yield online savings account. The down payment might be wisely stored in the higher-yielding CD.

But the point is that saving is best optimized, not maximized. There's a range in which a reasonable cash balance lies. Smart people stay squarely in it.

SUMMARY

1. Saving is stockpiling earned cash.
2. Saving erases worry and enables investing.
3. FDIC-insured high-yield online savings accounts house cash well.
4. Saving is always in the currency of one's expenses. Otherwise it's bad investing.
5. Neither CDs nor fixed income funds are ideal for savings.
6. Automatic savings plans increase the odds that one will have adequate savings.
7. Saving becomes excessive when it drifts into underinvesting.
8. The optimal amount of savings is a multiple of one's expenses.

CHAPTER 14

INVESTING

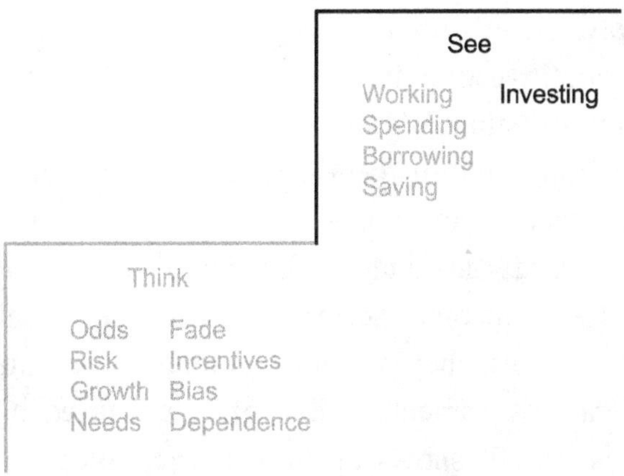

Investing is swapping some money now for more money later.

It's often how people get rich. And it's *always* part of how people *stay* rich.

Investing has three parts: assets, tactics, and accounts. They're all simple.

First is assets. We've seen how there are different asset classes: cash, fixed income securities, and stocks. And we know that they return differently. Cash returns modestly, fixed income securities return better, and stocks—listed stocks—return best.

It's straightforward to see why this ranking makes sense.

Take cash. It returns modestly because banks don't pay much interest. Sure, high-yield online savings accounts offer a bit more than traditional accounts. But not that much more. And yes, there are occasional periods when many banks pay well. But those times are rare.

Not even cash from other countries offers promise. There's just not much profit in foreign exchange. That's largely because currencies make up the largest financial market on earth. Dealing in euros, pounds, and dollars goes on every minute of every day. Traders around the world instantly bid low prices up and high prices down such that the microscopic gaps that occasionally surface shut immediately. There's no room to gain an edge.

In fact, returns from investing in cash are so modest, we usually don't even call it investing. We call it saving.

Fixed income securities return better. They return better because they pay more interest than bank accounts.

Plus, some come with tax advantages. *Municipal bonds*, for example. Those are fixed income securities issued by local governments like cities. *Munis*, they're called. Interest on munis isn't taxed by the federal government,[1] and is often not taxed by state governments. This benefit shows up in a metric called *tax equivalent yield*, which quantifies that bonus. We'll cover that later.

But still, bond returns aren't thrilling. That's because the money that can come from them is limited. It's limited to the promised interest, plus the repayment of principal. That's it. There's no jackpot. If a company has a great year, it doesn't give its bondholders a bonus.

There are exceptions. Some bonds trade on exchanges just like listed stocks. If a troubled company sees its fortunes improve, the price of its bonds can jump. That's because traders now see a decreased risk of default. Bondholders can then sell at a higher price and make real money.

But such situations aren't normal. The odds are against their happening. So bond returns are best seen as ceilinged.

Stocks are different. We've seen how stocks are ownership stakes in businesses. Businesses aren't restricted in how well they can do. They can develop new products, enter new markets, and impress customers. They can grow profits for decades.

Not all will, of course. But many do. That's why stocks perform best over time. Their prices reflect real commercial growth. They have no ceiling.

In short, the odds favor listed stocks. They've returned best in the past, and as ownership stakes in businesses without ceilings, should continue to do so.

Stocks in *privately held* companies are different. Those don't trade on exchanges. One could still try to buy some by negotiating with private companies directly. But that's rarely worth it. It takes real effort. Plus, too many of them fail. They just never reach critical mass.

Further, a private company willing to sell you stock may be *especially* likely to fail. That's why it's interested in your cash. It's desperate.

Private company investing provides a good example of *adverse selection*. That's a situation where the opportunities most available to you are precisely the ones you don't want.

Again, there are exceptions. Some angel investors have special relationships and skills. High-profile veteran entrepreneurs, for example. Quality startups want their investment because they're able to contribute their connections and know-how, making new ventures more likely to succeed.

But such people are outliers, not averages. If you're one of them, you know it. If you're not sure, you're not.

I'm not.

The second part of investing is tactics. Tactics are *ways* that people invest in assets like stocks. Tactics has a couple of aspects.

One is timing. It's about when to invest, and when to sell.

It's hard to predict when the stock market is about to tick up, or tick down. Impossible, really. So what many smart people do is invest automatically. They have their discount brokerage commit a set amount of dollars on the same date each month to a low-cost stock index fund.

Automatic investing has the happy effect of buying more of a fund when it's down. When the price of a fund is low, the same fixed amount of money buys more shares in the fund than when it's high. That's called *dollar cost averaging*.

To illustrate, say that in 2020 you automatically invested $1,000 on the last day of each month in a fund. The Schwab S&P 500 Index Fund, for example. You would have paid 12 different prices. At the end of January, you would have paid $49.37 per share. At the end of February, $45.31. And so on from March through December: $39.71, $44.80, $46.93, $47.87, $50.57, $54.20, $52.14, $50.75, $56.31, and $57.42.[2]

Adding those all up and dividing by 12 yields an average price of $49.62.

But you would have paid less. You would have paid only $49.08. That's because your $1,000 monthly budget would have bought you more shares on cheap days, and fewer shares on expensive days.

In March when the price was only $39.71, you would have loaded up on 25 shares. In December when it was $57.42, you would have scaled back to only 17:

http://www.smallstepstorich.com/14.1.xlsx

Smart people don't sell for the purpose of increasing returns. That's because they know they can't tell when the market has hit a high. So they don't try. They may sell part of a low-cost stock index fund to have enough cash to buy a house, pay tuition, or have more savings. But otherwise they hold. After all, it's only in retrospect that peaks look predictable.

Plus, tax law rewards holding. In the U.S. there's generally no tax owed on *unrealized* capital gains. If between January 1 and December 31 a fund goes up 10 percent, no capital gains tax is due for that year as long as none of the fund was sold. That's a great deal. It means that any amount that might have otherwise come out of the fund to pay the government instead gets to keep on growing. In America, tax law practically *begs* people to hold.

It doesn't everywhere, however. Some countries tax unrealized capital gains. They have a *wealth tax*. That's a periodic charge on net worth, including stock portfolios. Currently the only thing like that in the U.S. is *property tax*. That's a periodic charge on real estate holdings.

Another aspect of tactics is *passive versus active*. We saw this back in chapter 2. Passive management is about buying an index. Active management is about picking individual stocks. As we saw, passive beats active.

It's simple to see why this is so. Remember biases? Biases make punching bags out of active managers. The affinity bias tilts them toward unpromising firms hyped by telegenic CEOs. The anchoring bias pushes them to sell stock in perfectly fine companies just because prices momentarily dipped below cost. The consistency bias makes them hang on to stock they bought years ago in once-great businesses that have since faltered.

Passive managers are less susceptible to biases. That's because they have no big decisions to make. They just make sure that their holdings match those of the index. A well-trained cocker spaniel could do that.

That's one reason why low-cost stock index funds emerge as useful investments. Their managers sit a safe distance from the jabs of human misjudgment.

A fund that is low cost has, by definition, a low *expense ratio*. That reflects how much it costs a financial institution to run the fund.

An expense ratio is a percentage. It comes in two flavors: *gross* and *net*.

The *gross expense ratio* is all the annual operating expenses of the fund divided by the amount of money in the fund.

Sometimes a financial institution gives investors a discount. It picks up some of the operating expenses of the fund instead of passing them all along to investors. That nicety is captured in the *net expense ratio*. It's the annual operating expenses of the fund, less fee waivers and reimbursements; divided by the amount of money in the fund.

Both ratios matter. The net expense ratio is what investors actually pay. But the discount it reflects can go away. The freebies can vanish. If they do, the net expense ratio becomes the gross expense ratio. So it's good to know how tight a ship the institution runs since that may eventually come to influence actual returns.

Some funds also quote an *adjusted expense ratio*. It's equal to or lower than the net expense ratio. That's because it leaves out an additional category of costs, costs that come from certain kinds of financial gymnastics. The details of those gymnastics aren't important. What is important is that the adjusted expense ratio makes some funds look better.

I appreciate the rationale behind the adjusted expense ratio. It strips away costs related to trading strategies, not operating efficiency.[3] But I'm suspicious of it. Those trading expenses are real. So if I had to hang my hat on a single cost number it would still be the gross expense ratio.

Good low-cost stock index funds are based on any of several standard indexes. The most popular is the S&P 500. It's a collection of *large caps*, or stocks in big corporations. It's the one behind the Schwab S&P 500 Index Fund that we saw earlier.

The S&P 500 is *capitalization-weighted.* That means that the percentage of the index allocated to each stock is different. It varies with *market capitalization.*

Market capitalization is the theoretical price of all of a company's shares. It's the number of shares times the share price. It's often called *market cap.*

The higher a corporation's market cap, the more of the S&P 500 it constitutes. As of this writing, company number one makes up over 6 percent of the S&P 500. Company number 500, by contrast, makes up around one-hundredth of 1 percent.[4]

An alternative is the *S&P 500 Equal Weight* index. It's not capitalization-weighted. Instead, the percentage of the index allocated to each corporation is the same.[5]

An entirely different index is the *Russell 3000.* It's another capitalization-weighted collection of American large caps.[6]

Which standard stock market index is going to outperform the others? The S&P 500, S&P 500 Equal Weight, or the Russell 3000? I have no idea. But I do think that they'll all outperform both most stock pickers and other asset classes over time.

Low-cost stock index funds take two forms: *mutual funds* and *exchange-traded funds*.

Mutual funds trade just once a day. To buy them, one places a *market order*. One can decide how much to invest, but not what price per share to pay. The order simply transacts at the market price—whatever that turns out to be—at the end of the day.

But exchange traded funds—also called *ETF*s—trade continuously throughout the day. One can buy them with a *limit order*. One can decide how much to invest, and the price at which to invest. Only if the market price drops to that level will the order execute.

ETFs have some other advantages as well. For one, they're tax efficient. They trigger a tax liability on dividends, just like mutual funds. But they generally don't trigger capital gains taxes until they're sold. This is in contrast to mutual funds, which regularly trigger capital gains taxes because of the way that they're structured. In addition, ETFs often have lower expense ratios. They're cheaper to administer, which translates into fewer costs cutting into investors' returns.

The big drawback of ETFs is that they're harder to use for automatic investing. For that, one generally needs mutual funds.

Each mutual fund has a unique *ticker symbol*. It identifies the mutual fund on a stock exchange. It's five letters, the last of which is X. For example, the Schwab S&P 500 Index Fund is a mutual fund. Its ticker symbol is SWPPX.

Each ETF also has a unique ticker symbol. It's between two and four letters, the last of which can be anything.

A fund has many statistics. A handful of them are useful. The expense ratios, for example. Another is the *NAV*. That stands for *net asset value*. It's the worth of each fund share from a strict accounting standpoint. It's usually equal—or darn close—to the share price, as you might expect.

An additional statistic is the *distribution yield*. It sizes up the payments—*distributions*—that a fund makes to its shareholders. It's a ratio. The numerator is distributions per share over the last 12 months. The denominator is NAV at the end of those 12 months. Distribution yield is sometimes called *trailing 12-months yield* or *TTM yield*.

A similar metric is the *30-day SEC yield*. It's also a ratio. On top is dividends and interest received by the fund, minus the fund's operating expenses. That top is an annualized take on what actually happened during the most recent full month. On the bottom is the highest price of the fund's shares on the last day of that month.

Incidentally, *SEC* stands for *Securities and Exchange Commission*. That's the U.S. government agency that regulates securities markets.

The distribution yield and the 30-day SEC yield are useful when the priority is *income*. They help to predict how much cash a fund might pay out each year. But income is rarely the priority with stock funds. Instead, the priority is *appreciation*. It's about how much each share goes up in price over the long term.

Where income becomes the priority is with fixed income funds. Those can be useful to own in retirement. So we'll return to the metrics of distribution yield and the 30-day SEC yield in chapter 21.

A final useful fund statistic is *AAR*. That stands for *average annual return*. It takes a comprehensive look at the past performance of the fund. It's the single rate of return that, had it been achieved each year, would have delivered the same end result that the more volatile annual returns actually did.

A fund generally presents AARs for 1, 3, 5, and 10-year periods. It also shows one for all of the time that has passed since the fund started, or *since inception*. The longer the period, the more telling the AAR. That's because longer periods smooth out short-term volatility. To the long-term investor, that's useful.

AARs are calculated net of a fund's operating costs. Those are the costs that we first saw in the expense ratios. So AARs give a pretty clear view of what actually happened.

AARs are not, however, net of taxes. That's because different people have different tax rates. Their incomes put them in different federal tax brackets. Their locations give them different state and local taxes. And the accounts in which they hold funds could be taxable, tax-deferred, or tax-free. So it would be impossible for fund companies to present after-tax returns that apply in all cases.

But fund companies do present supplementary tables with hypothetical after-tax returns. They do this by making assumptions. Generally, they assume the top individual federal income tax rates in effect at the time of each distribution, and don't consider state and local taxes.

Tactics are not to be confused with *strategies*. In the world of investing, strategies refers to methods of active management. There are basically three: growth, momentum, and value.

Growth centers on buying assets likely to increase in worth. Momentum emphasizes buying assets that just increased in price, on the belief that they'll continue to increase in price. Value focuses on buying assets for less than worth.

Actively managed funds often launch under the banner of one of these three strategies. But which strategy flag a fund flies matters less than the buzzkilling truth that active managers routinely get trounced by their passive counterparts.

The third part of investing is accounts. We've seen how work provides the opportunity to invest through accounts that have special advantages.

A 401(k), for example. Contributions to a 401(k) are tax deductible, and employers often match those contributions. That's a great deal.

A drawback to 401(k) plans is that the funds one can invest in through them are limited. They're limited to the funds offered by the financial institution that manages the employer's retirement plans. Perhaps instead of a low-cost stock index fund, the institution only offers a stock index fund that charges a high 1 percent annual fee.

This problem disappears with an IRA. That's a different kind of advantaged account. We've seen how traditional IRAs offer tax savings when money goes in, and Roth IRAs offer tax savings when money comes out. Both are useful. And the funds one can invest in through them are usually better. They make it easy to use a low-cost stock index fund.

In fact, it's sensible to select a discount brokerage partly based on the quality of its IRA fund offerings. In 2022 discount brokerages worth considering include Fidelity, Schwab, and Vanguard. They're able to meet so many of their clients' needs that it's hard to see full-service brokerages as adding anything other than cost.

Amounts held at brokerages aren't insured in the way that amounts held at banks are insured by the FDIC. But they are backed by the *SIPC*. That's the *Securities Investor Protection Corporation*. It's a non-profit corporation that helps clients retrieve their assets if a brokerage becomes distressed.[7]

Advantaged accounts like 401(k)s and IRAs have annual contribution limits. So the bulk of a smart person's investments often aren't in them. Instead, they're in normal, taxable brokerage accounts. Those are available from the same discount brokerages that offer IRAs. There's nothing wrong with taxable brokerage accounts provided that full use is first made of advantaged accounts.

Many people invest through a financial advisor. Those professionals commonly charge an annual fee of around 1 percent of *assets under management*. That doesn't sound like much. But it adds up. It could clip the average annual return from a low-cost stock index fund from 7 percent to 6 percent. The difference over 30 years would look like this:

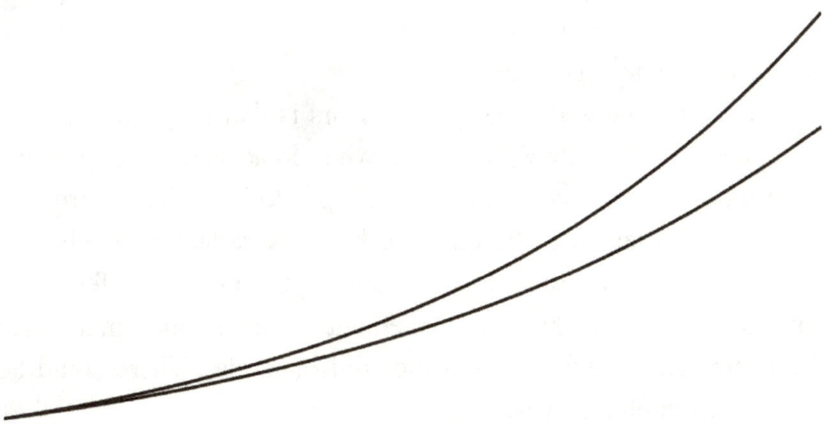

The upper curve shows growth without the advisor, and the lower curve shows growth with the advisor.

Please look at the far right edge of the picture. Notice that one could wind up with just three-quarters of what one would have without the advisor. That's like hiring a personal trainer to injure you.

The same bad result could come from investing in a fund that charges a 1 percent annual fee as opposed to a vanishingly small fee. One could wind up with just three-quarters of what one deserves.

Of course if a financial advisor delivered better returns than did a low-cost stock index fund, things would be different. One would happily pay 1 percent for an annual average return of, say, 9 percent. But we've seen how the odds are against that happening.

It gets uglier. Picture an advisor that charges a 1 percent annual fee to put clients into a stock index fund that itself charges a 1 percent annual fee. The client's net average annual return could then be slashed to 5 percent. And if the fund is active instead of passive, the net return could get so low that cash could start to look attractive.

Even worse is a *wrap fee*. It's a single price charged by a financial advisor that covers incidentals like brokerage costs in addition to advisory services. It's also an annual percent of assets under management. There's nothing wrong with it in theory. But it can be as high as 3 percent.

Another issue with financial advisors is that they can increase dependence. They may construct what look like custom stock portfolios. But the contents of such portfolios often mirror an index. They pretend to be tailored, but they're standard. They're *closet indexes*. The only extra is the 1 percent annual fee. And since such portfolios have more elements than a holding in a single fund, they could make leaving the advisor harder. There could be increased switching costs.

Nonetheless, advisors take steps to portray themselves as authorities. They flaunt their designations. For example:

Kenneth Jeffrey Marshall, MBA, CFRB

Pretty impressive, right? Don't be fooled.

MBA just means that I finished graduate school. While there I wasn't required to take a single money management class.

And *CFRB?* That's an AM radio station in Toronto.

In fairness, some designations are relevant. *RIA*, for example. That stands for *registered investment advisor*. Another is *CFP*. That stands for *certified financial planner*.

RIAs and CFPs are *fiduciaries*.[8] That means that they've committed to putting their clients' interests ahead of their own. That's good. It brings the advisors' incentives closer to the clients' incentives.

Another relevant designation is *fee-only*. It identifies advisors that are paid only by clients. That's also good.

By contrast *fee-based* identifies advisors that may also be paid by providers of investment products. That can motivate them to recommend expensive, underperforming funds. That's bad. It drives the advisors' incentives away from the clients' incentives.

One function of an advisor is to determine *asset allocation*. That's how much of a client's wealth is in stocks, how much is in cash, and how much is in fixed income securities. But none of that is particularly hard to do.

Plus, it's gotten easier. Automated solutions now exist. *Target-date funds*, for example. They automatically determine sensible asset allocations based largely on a client's age. Provided that they're low cost, store cash safely, and use low-cost index funds, they can work well. They're available from discount brokerages.

Two activities routinely masquerade as investing. Knowing about them lowers risk.

The first is spending. The three asset classes we've focused on are cash, fixed income securities, and stocks. But there's a fourth: *real assets*. They're physical. They derive their worth from tangibility. They include real estate like farmland, metals like silver, and commodities like oil. As a group they tend over the long term to return more than cash but less than listed stocks.

A problem with real assets is that they can justify giving in to wants. We may want a vintage guitar, or an antique chair. Goods like that could be considered real assets, and may be described by sellers as investments. They tempt us to envision a return.

But the odds are that returns from guitars or chairs will disappoint. Plus in strumming or sitting, we consume. Such buys are therefore best seen as spending.

The second activity that masquerades as investing is speculating. That's purchasing something in the hope that it can be sold at a higher price later, with no consideration as to why that may be possible. An example is buying a cryptocurrency for the sole purpose of flipping it to another speculator.

Investing and saving are similar. Both are about accumulating wealth, and properly housing that wealth. But they differ in their relationship to volatility.

In saving, volatility is bad. It's unacceptable for any amount of stockpiled cash to become unavailable, even for an hour. It all has to always be there. That's why high-yield online accounts make so much sense for savings. The price never fluctuates.

But in investing, volatility is fine. It's not only normal, it's advantageous. It's advantageous because if stock prices are down on an automatic investing day, you score more shares in a low-cost stock index fund. That's the power of dollar cost averaging.

Investing really is straightforward. Seen properly, it has only the three parts of assets, tactics, and accounts. Seen wrongly, it has many more. But smart people keep their vision simple because anything else is likely to stunt returns.

SUMMARY

1. Investing is swapping some money now for more money later.
2. Investing is often how people get rich, and always part of how they stay rich.
3. The three parts of investing are assets, tactics, and accounts.
4. Listed stocks tend to return better over time than other asset classes.
5. Passive stock funds tend to outperform active stock funds over time.
6. Low-cost stock index funds come in two forms: mutual funds and ETFs.
7. Automated investing harnesses the power of dollar cost averaging.
8. What financial advisors and full-service brokerages reliably add is fees.
9. Spending and speculating often masquerade as investing.
10. Volatility is unacceptable in saving, but advantageous in investing.

CHAPTER 15

INSURING

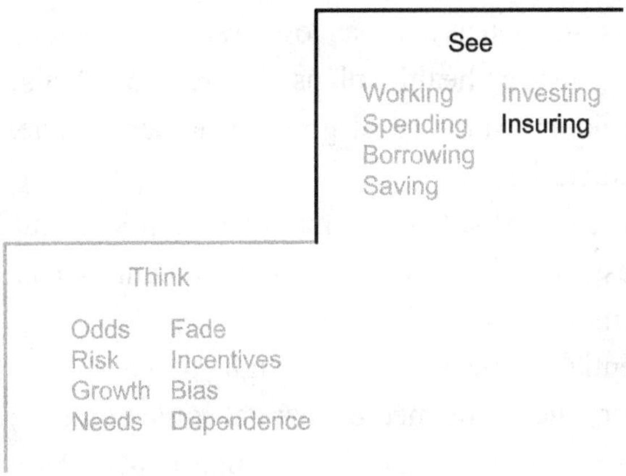

Insuring lowers risk.

It complements investing. Investing delivers returns, while insuring mitigates losses.

There are good insurance policies, and bad insurance policies. Good policies lower risk a lot, inexpensively. Bad policies lower risk a little, expensively.

Those are the extremes, obviously. But they're useful to define because they mark the endpoints of the spectrum on which all policies lie.

Consider a good insurance policy. It has four characteristics.

First, the potential expense it offloads is massive. Without coverage, one might personally incur big costs.

Second, the potential expense has a high probability of happening.

Third, the policy comes from a financially sound insurer. The company has a high rating from a recognized agency like A.M. Best, Fitch, Moody's, or S&P. A high rating increases the odds that a valid claim will be paid.

Ratings aren't perfect. Sometimes highly-rated insurers come to have difficulties. But poorly-rated ones more often do. So if an insurer has a low rating, there's no point in becoming its client.

Fourth, the policy is inexpensive. It has low *premiums*, or fees.

In 2022 I'd characterize health plans offered by Kaiser Permanente in California as examples of good insurance policies. They have all four characteristics.

First, the expenses they offload can be massive. That's because American medical costs are high, and the government doesn't provide all of its citizens with health insurance.

Second, the potential expense has a high probability of happening. Almost everyone needs medical care at some point.

Third, the plans come from a financially sound entity. As of this writing Kaiser has a high AA- rating from Fitch,[1] and doesn't have a low rating from any agency. Plus Kaiser actually owns the hospitals and clinics that provide the covered services, making it even more likely that it will fulfill its obligations.

Finally, the policies are relatively inexpensive, with premiums that are among the lowest in California.

Of course some people don't need Kaiser health insurance. They get coverage through work, or through a government program like Medicare. Others don't like Kaiser because it has a limited—however large—pool of doctors. And I must confess that I've never been a Kaiser customer myself, and as such have no first-hand experience to relate.

But on balance a Kaiser health plan looks like a good insurance policy. For many it lowers risk a lot, inexpensively.

A bad insurance policy also has four characteristics.

First, the potential expenses it offloads are trivial. They're small enough that one could pay for them out of pocket.

Second, the potential expenses have low odds of happening.

Third, the policy comes from a shaky carrier. The insurance company has a low rating, suggesting that even valid claims might not be paid.

Fourth, it's expensive. The premium is high relative to what's covered.

While an insurance policy with all four of these characteristics is certainly bad, one with three or fewer can be bad as well. An extended warranty on a smartphone, for example.

One consumer electronics company includes a one-year warranty on all of its new smartphones. If the phone breaks during the first year, the company will replace it. But for an additional fee —a premium—the company will extend the warranty for a second year.

The new smartphone costs $549. The premium is $64. There's a $79 *deductible* charged to the policyholder if a claim is paid.

Understandably, the policy has some conditions. No more than two claims can be filed during the year. Theft isn't covered. And a claim won't be honored if the phone was dropped, dunked underwater, or exposed to extreme temperatures. So no skydiving into hot tubs.

Some simple math makes clear whether or not the extended warranty is useful.

The new smartphone price of $549 minus the deductible of $79 equals $470. So that's the value of a valid claim. It would be the net payout. Easy.

The big question centers on odds. What's the probability that the smartphone will break in a way that's covered during its second year?

One can't know for sure. But maybe 10 percent? Let's try that.

Ten percent times the net payout of $470 equals $47. So the *expected value* of the policy is -$17. That's just $47 minus the premium of $64. And it's negative. So if our assumptions are correct, we're looking at a policy that's bad.

If the premium were lower, it might make sense. Less than $47, to be exact, since then the policy would have a positive expected value. But as it stands the policy is expensive relative to what's covered.

Further, the $549 replacement cost might not be enough to merit any insurance at all. For many, it's an amount that could easily be paid out of pocket.

Plus, the replacement cost might actually be lower. New smartphone models come out all the time. And when they do, the price of older models plunge. So by the time one had to buy a replacement, the price might be just $500, or $400, or even less.

But by that point one might not want to replace an older-model smartphone at all. One might want a newer model.

So the policy looks bad both because the potential expense it offloads is small, and because it's expensive. In fact, extended warranties on many goods—home appliances, laptops, TVs—wind up looking like that.

Now consider life insurance for someone without dependents.

A life insurance policy pays money to designated people—called *beneficiaries*—when the insured dies. The payout is called, charmingly, a *death benefit*.

But if there are no dependents, it's not clear who the beneficiaries should be. If someone doesn't support a spouse or children, life insurance wouldn't seem to be necessary. That's because the odds that dependents will need financial help are zero. There aren't any.

Of course many people do support dependents, and rely on their earned income to do so. Smart people in this situation often choose *level term* life insurance.

Level means that both the premiums and the death benefit remain the same over the life of the policy. *Term* means that the policy lasts only for a set number of years, presumably for as long as the dependents need support. Thirty years is common.

Other forms of life insurance look worse. They include *universal life* and *whole life*. Their shared drawback is that they have investment components. In addition to lowering risk, they promise returns. But the odds are that such returns will lag those of a low-cost stock index fund.

Insurers offer other investment products as well. *Annuities*, for example. They take cash payments up front, and make payouts later. There's nothing wrong with them in principle. But again, they tend to return less than do low-cost stock index funds.

Insurance companies are best seen as sources of lower risk, not of higher returns. Smart people don't go to them for investments any more than they go to dentists for manicures. Insuring and investing are intelligently viewed as distinct activities.

Good insurance policies can often be made better. Consider homeowners insurance. It can be made better by changing settlement terms.

Homeowners policies pay for losses on property, including furniture. Often they pay *actual cash value*. That's cost minus *depreciation*. So if living room furniture expected to last for 10 years cost $10,000; and it's destroyed five years later; the insurer might only pay $5,000.

But not if the settlement term is *replacement cost*. That requires the insurer to pay for new, comparable furniture. There would be a deductible, and a higher premium. But if the goal is to lower the chance that one will ever have to pay to replace destroyed property, replacement cost may be the better settlement term.

Another way good insurance policies can be made better is with lower premiums. Those can be secured in a couple of ways.

One way is by eliminating unnecessary coverages. Take auto insurance. It typically has both a *liability* component and a *collision and comprehensive* component.

The liability component is essential. It covers damage caused to other people and property. In the event of an accident, those numbers can be big.

But the collision and comprehensive component just covers damage to the insured's car. It's useful if the car would be expensive to replace. Same if the car was bought with a loan that still has an outstanding balance. In that case the collision and comprehensive component should cover the amount still owed.

But if the car wouldn't be expensive to replace and there's no outstanding loan, perhaps collision and comprehensive coverage isn't necessary.

I cancelled mine in 2011. That year Kelly Blue Book—the authority on used car prices in the U.S.—estimated the value of my once-glorious 1998 Saab 900S turbo at just $1,800.

At first I was offended. But then I felt lucky. After all, I could pay $1,800 out of pocket. So I stripped collision and comprehensive out of my policy and got a meaningful reduction in my premium.

Incidentally, this highlights an advantage of not regularly buying new luxury vehicles. One saves on insurance.

Another way premiums can be lowered is by increasing deductibles. If one has enough cash to easily cover some out-of-pocket costs, then higher deductibles may be a good way to increase a policy's expected value.

For example, consider an *HDHP*. That's short for *High Deductible Health Plan.* It's health insurance with an annual deductible of at least some minimum. In 2022 that minimum is $1,400 for an individual and $2,800 for a family.[2]

Predictably, HDHPs have lower premiums than more standard policies. Plus, they qualify the policyholder to contribute to an *HSA*. That's short for *Health Savings Account*. It's an advantaged account that's available from discount brokerages.

Annual contributions to an HSA are tax deductible up to a limit. In 2022 that limit is $3,650 for an individual and $7,300 for a family. Those contributions could be invested in a low-cost stock index fund, and the returns won't be taxed. Not even withdrawals will be taxed as long as they're used to pay for *qualified* medical expenses.

Qualified just means allowed by rule.

Qualified medical expenses include deductibles, *copayments*, and *coinsurance*. Copayments are smaller fixed amounts paid by a policyholder for medical services. Coinsurance—an equally riveting novelty—is the percentage of the cost of a medical service borne by a policyholder beyond the deductible.

HDHP premiums, however, aren't qualified medical expenses.

When HSAs really start to shine is past age 65. That's when the balance can be withdrawn for non-medical purposes without penalty. The withdrawals are subject to income tax, as with traditional IRAs. But someone who started making contributions early, invested those contributions well, and stayed basically healthy could wind up with an HSA balance that's considerable.

For this reason some see an HSA as a bonus IRA. They choose an HDHP primarily to get the HSA. There's a logic to that.

But it can backfire for someone who winds up needing a lot of medical care. That's because HDHPs have high annual out-of-pocket maximums. That's the most in deductibles, copays, and coinsurance that a policyholder is responsible for each year. In 2022 those maximums are $7,050 for an individual and $14,100 for a family.[3]

Obviously, an HDHP wouldn't work for someone with a chronic medical condition. The out-of-pocket expenses would dwarf the advantaged account benefits. What's tough is for someone who's healthy to predict whether or not they could develop such a condition. When you're well, it's hard to see yourself sick.

Insurance is often bought through insurance agents. But other sources can be better. Organizations, for example. One's employer, a spouse's employer, alumni associations, and affinity groups often offer attractive deals.

Another promising source is direct insurers. They sell straight to individuals instead of through agents. They're like discount brokerages in investing. In auto, for example, they include Progressive and Geico (in whose parent I am a shareholder).

Insurance needs change as net worth increases. For example, deductibles can be set higher. Filing a claim is bothersome, and a rich person's savings may be sufficient to easily pay for small losses. So raising deductibles can both spare one hassles and reduce premiums.

In addition, an *umbrella* insurance policy may become advisable. It provides excess liability coverage. For example, an auto policy supplies liability coverage only up to a specified maximum. After that, the umbrella policy takes over. That's useful because a rich person has more wealth to protect.

Some insurance coverages are needs: liability for auto, umbrella once you have a sizable net worth, and health always.

But many aren't. They're unnecessary. In fact some can be made unnecessary by not doing things that would require insurance in the first place.

I've never been a gambler, as you might expect. But my UCLA years were peppered with road trips to skiing in Colorado that occasioned stopovers in Las Vegas.

Watching my classmates at the blackjack table, I saw how a dealer showing an ace would often offer "insurance." That gave players the chance to wager half of their original bet on the dealer having a blackjack, or cards adding up to 21. If the dealer did, the payout was twice the wager.

I didn't expect a prudent insurance offer to surface in the wee hours of a casino. But my nature is such that I ran the math anyway.

An ace is worth 11. So for the dealer to have 21, the other card would have to be a 10. What are the chances of that?

Well, let's see. There are four suits: clubs, diamonds, hearts, and spades. Each has a 10 card. So that's four 10s right there.

Plus each suit has three face cards: jack, queen, and king. Each of those is also worth 10. Four suits times three face cards equals 12. Twelve plus four is 16. So a deck has 16 cards worth 10.

A deck has 52 cards. But only 51 are hidden, since the dealer's ace is already showing. So the probability that the dealer's other card is a 10 is 16 divided by 51. That's about 31 percent.

The payout is twice the wager. So if the wager—the premium—is $100, the payout would be $200. Thirty-one percent times $200 is $62. So the expected value of the policy is -$38. That's $62 minus $100. And it's negative.

Instead of reducing the chance of loss, the policy increases it. Smart people wouldn't see that as insurance. What would they see as insurance?

Leaving the casino.

SUMMARY

1. Insuring lowers risk.
2. Good insurance lowers risk a lot, inexpensively.
3. Bad insurance lowers risk a little, expensively.
4. Good insurance may be made better by changing settlement terms, eliminating unnecessary coverage, and raising deductibles.
5. Good insurance deals often come from organizations and direct insurers.
6. Umbrella insurance becomes more useful as one gets wealthier.

CHAPTER 16

PLANNING

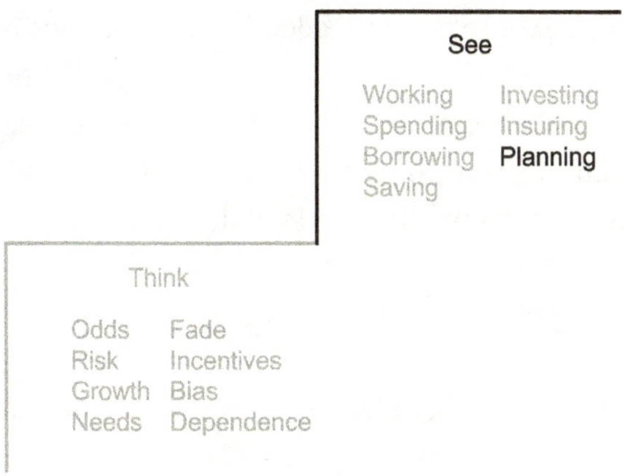

No one lives forever. So smart people do *estate planning*. They arrange in advance how they want their assets distributed once they've passed. *Estate* just means net worth. It's what you own, minus what you owe.

The goal of estate planning is simple. It's to send as much of your net worth as possible where you want it to go, without turning your heirs into listless slobs.

That last bit I can't do much about. It hinges more on personality and upbringing than anything that I can influence. But the first bit—sending as much of your net worth as possible where you want it to go—is straightforward. It's about minimizing taxes, and avoiding *probate*.

Minimizing taxes mostly means minimizing *estate taxes*. Those get paid out of an estate before it's distributed to heirs.

Fortunately, federal estate taxes kick in only above a certain threshold. That threshold changes. But in 2021 it was $11,700,000. That's called the *basic exclusion amount*.

That $11,700,000 is per individual. So a married couple's estate exclusion was doubled to $23,400,000. And the unused exclusion of a deceased spouse can pass to the surviving spouse.[1]

Most estates are smaller than the basic exclusion amount. But some are bigger. That can expose them to federal estate tax rates of up to 40 percent.[2]

Plus some states want their cut as well. In 2021, 11 states had an estate tax: Connecticut, Hawaii, Illinois, Maine, Massachusetts, Minnesota, New York, Oregon, Rhode Island, Vermont and Washington, plus Washington, D.C.

State estate tax can apply even if federal estate tax doesn't. That's because state basic exclusions are lower. In 2021 they ranged from $1,000,000 in Massachusetts[3] and Oregon[4] to $5,930,000 in New York.[5]

State estate tax rates can be material. In Hawaii[6] and Washington[7] they went all the way up to 20 percent. Thankfully, most aren't nearly that high. But because they kick in at a lower threshold, they matter.

All of this can make it useful to lessen the size of an estate. So some smart people start transferring assets while they're still alive. They make *gifts*. They get a head start doling out wealth to heirs, heirs that will ultimately get the estate anyway. That reduces the amount that will eventually get clipped by taxes.

Gifts are best made without triggering *gift taxes*. Those are assessed on wealth given away. Luckily, they're easy to avoid. Just limit what you gift. Since 2018 you can give up to $15,000 per year, per *donee* without owing federal taxes. That's called the *gift tax exclusion*.[8]

Donee is just the IRS's term for recipient.

Gift taxes are mostly a federal matter. In 2021 the only state with a gift tax was Connecticut.[9]

There's no limit on the number of donees a donor can gift to each year. Someone with 10 donees—like 4 children and 6 grandchildren—could transfer a total of $150,000 in 2021 without owing gift tax.

A couple could gift twice as much. They could give a total of $30,000 in 2021 per donee. That's because each partner gets their own gift tax exclusion.

If a gift is made in cash, its value is clear. After all, a dollar is a dollar. So a donor that transferred $15,000 in cash to a donee in 2021 obviously wouldn't owe any gift tax.

Same with shares listed on a stock exchange. VOO, for example. That's the ticker symbol for Vanguard's S&P 500 ETF.[10] If a donor gave 50 shares to one donee when VOO traded at $300, the donor wouldn't owe any gift tax. That's because 50 times $300 is $15,000. Again, the value of the gift is clear.

But sometimes it isn't. Take real estate. The value of real estate for gift tax purposes is the *fair market value*. That's an estimate. It's the price at which a buyer and seller would willingly exchange a property, assuming that both knew the property well and weren't under any pressure to close a deal. It can be hard to gauge. So some donors and donees hire an *appraiser* to calculate it.

If a donor bought some land in 1970 for $14,000 and gifted it to a donee in 2021 when its fair market value was $50,000, gift tax could apply to $35,000. That's just the fair market value minus the gift tax exclusion of $15,000. The $14,000 purchase price would be irrelevant. It would become relevant, however, if the donee subsequently sold the land. That's because the donor's *basis* would become the donee's basis.[11]

To illustrate, say that after buying the land in 1970 the donor didn't alter the property. The donor's basis would then be the purchase price of $14,000. It would be the same as the *cost basis*. If in 2022 the donee sold the land for $50,000, the donee would have a capital gain of $36,000. That's just the selling price minus the basis.

Let's twist this a little. Say that the donor did alter the property. Right before gifting, the donor installed a fence around the land at a cost of $2,000. The basis would then ratchet up to $16,000. That would be the *adjusted basis*. It's the original purchase price plus the cost of the improvement.

If right after receiving the property the donee then sold it for $50,000, the capital gain would be only $34,000. The adjusted basis would have passed from donor to donee.

Also passing from donor to donee is the *holding period*. That's the time since the donor bought the property. The donee inherits the donor's starting date.

A holding period over a year results in a *long-term capital gain*. A holding period of a year or less results in a *short-term capital gain*. That matters because tax rates on long-term capital gains are generally lower than on short-term capital gains.

Our example shows us a long-term capital gain. That's so even if the donee sold the land right after receiving it, since 1970 was well over a year ago.

There are plenty of wrinkles to gifted real estate. There's depreciation, the impact of gift tax on basis, and the freak situation of a property's fair market value dropping below adjusted basis. But the point is this: basis transfers from donor to donee.

It doesn't, however, when real estate transfers after the owner dies. Instead, *stepped-up basis* applies. That's the fair market value of the property when it transfers from estate to heir.

Consider again the land bought in 1970 for $14,000. Say that the owner dies in 2022, and an heir gets the property when its fair market value is $50,000. If the heir sells a month later for $60,000, the capital gain is only $10,000. That's because the heir's stepped-up basis is $50,000. The deceased's basis—adjusted or otherwise—wouldn't matter.

It gets better. That $10,000 would be a long-term capital gain, even though the heir owned it for just a month. That's because any property received in an inheritance is assumed to have been held for more than a year for tax purposes.[12]

All of this explains why real estate is often the last asset that smart people gift. It appreciates. Better to let it go to heirs after death, when it comes accessorized with a handy stepped-up basis. No wonder smart people start gifting with cash, where there's no gap between basis and fair market value.

Gift taxes aren't as limiting as they might first seem. That's because an individual can usually gift more than $15,000 per donee in a single year without triggering them. Excess amounts simply reduce, dollar for dollar, the estate tax basic exclusion amount.

To illustrate, say that in 2021 someone had never given more than the annual gift tax exclusion. Their estate still had the full $11,700,000 exclusion waiting for it. If they gave $715,000 to one donee, their federal basic exclusion amount would drop to $11,000,000. That's just the starting basic exclusion amount of $11,700,000 minus the gift amount over $15,000.

Stated differently, the federal estate tax basic exclusion amount can be gradually used up over a lifetime.

It gets better for married couples. Recall that their basic exclusion amount is twice that of an individual. So in 2021 it was $23,400,000. And that doubling doesn't disappear when one spouse dies. The unused exclusion can pass to the surviving spouse. It's *portable*. It's called a *DSUE*, for *deceased spousal unused exclusion*. In 2021 it let a surviving spouse give up to $23,400,000 without triggering any gift taxes.

Transferring a DSUE requires an *election*. That means that action is required. Specifically, IRS Form 706 has to be filled out and submitted on time.[13]

Most gifts can be used by donees as they wish. But not all. Take gifts to a *custodial account*. That's an account that's owned by a minor but run by an adult. The minor only gets access to it in adulthood. Usually that's defined as starting at age 18.

Gifts to a *529 plan* are similar. They can only be used to pay for school.

Discount brokerages offer 529 accounts. They're somewhat similar to Roth IRAs. For example, contributions to them aren't tax deductible. Returns earned on those contributions aren't taxed while they're in the 529. And amounts withdrawn from them aren't taxed as long as they're used to pay for textbooks, tuition, or other qualified education expenses.[14]

States administer 529 plans. There are actually two kinds. The more common one—the one sketched out above—is the *education savings plan*.

The other is the *prepaid tuition plan*. It lets donors pay a donee's tuition years in advance, before inflation has had a chance to ply its sorcery.

Prepaid tuition plans may be on the way out. As of 2022, only nine states still offer them. That's probably just as well, since they can limit the range of schools that make sense for a donee to attend.[15] They increase dependence.

Some gifts are never taxed. They can never cut into the basic exclusion amount.

Gifts to a spouse, for example. They're not subject to gift tax provided that the spouse is a U.S. citizen. And even if the spouse isn't a citizen, there's no gift tax on transfers up to a pretty high level. In 2021 that level was $159,000 per year.[16]

Healthcare is similar. Someone paying a medical bill on behalf of a donee doesn't owe gift tax provided that the amount is paid directly to the medical institution, care provider, or health insurer.[17]

Same with school. Someone paying tuition on behalf of a donee isn't taxed, as long as the amount is paid directly to the educational institution.[18]

This exposes something curious about 529 plans. Contributions to them count towards the gift tax exclusion. But tuition paid by a donor doesn't. So families that don't have a 529 plan still have a tax-efficient way to pay for education.

Separate from estate tax is *inheritance tax*. It's assessed on amounts received from an estate. It's paid by heirs.

There's no inheritance tax at the federal level. That's good. And as of 2022 there are only six states that levy inheritance taxes: Iowa, Kentucky, Maryland, Nebraska, New Jersey, and Pennsylvania.

But state inheritance taxes are based on the whereabouts of the deceased, not the heir. If the deceased lived or owned real estate in one of those six states, inheritance taxes could apply. For example a Californian inheriting a farm in Nebraska might get a bill from the Cornhusker State.

Maximum state inheritance tax rates range from 10 percent in Maryland[19] to 18 percent in Nebraska.[20] There are plenty of exemptions, based both on amounts and one's relationship to the deceased. So the effective rates are usually much lower. But they're still real.

Tax considerations are worth weighing. But don't go overboard. One shouldn't let the tax tail wag the life dog. Minimizing taxes in a way that brings unhappiness would be silly.

For example, Alaska has no state gift tax, no estate tax, and no inheritance tax. It doesn't even have sales or income tax.[21] Should you move there? If you love Alaska, sure. But if you don't, no.

One reason not to obsess over taxes is that they change. Consider the federal estate tax basic exclusion amount. In 2021 it was $11,700,000, as noted. But in 2017 it was only $5,490,000.[22] It's actually slated to slide back towards that level in 2026.[23] And maybe it will. But who knows?

Incidentally, if the basic exclusion amount does revert, people who made large gifts in earlier years won't be penalized. For example, say that someone made their first-ever gift in 2021. Say it was $10,000,000 to one donee. Their federal basic exclusion amount would then get cut to $1,715,000. That's just $11,700,000 minus $10,000,000, plus the gift tax exclusion of $15,000. If in 2026 the federal basic exclusion amount drops to $5,490,000—well under their $10,000,000 gift—they won't be retroactively charged.[24]

The other major part of estate planning is avoiding *probate*. Probate is a messy legal process for sorting out who gets what after you pass. It's a murky circus of court, costs, and legalese. Your heirs would find it stressful, expensive, and time consuming.

Fortunately, it's easy to skip. While avoiding probate is generally thought of as the domain of attorneys, much of it can be tackled with the basic tools of personal finance.

For example, most accounts can be made *ITF.* That stands for *in trust for*. It's sometimes called *POD*, for the adorable *payable on death.* Assets in ITF and POD accounts automatically go to your beneficiaries when you die.

CMAs (cash management accounts), MMAs (money market accounts), IRAs, bank accounts, and stock brokerage accounts can all be made ITF. Many financial institutions even allow you to designate different percentages of an account to different heirs. It's all done easily, and usually online.

Some assets don't come with ready ITF mechanisms. Homes, for example. So for them, smart people set up *trusts*. Those are legal entities established to own assets like houses so that they too can pass straight to heirs.

Trusts are easy to understand. They have three parties: *grantor*, *trustee*, and *beneficiary*.

A *grantor* contributes assets to the trust, like a home. It's probably you. A grantor is sometimes called a *trustor* or *settlor*.

A *trustee* manages the trust. The person who is the grantor can also be the trustee.

A *beneficiary* ultimately receives the assets in the trust. That's similar to ITF accounts. And as with ITF accounts, a trust can have more than one beneficiary.

There are different kinds of trusts. A type commonly used to own homes is a *living trust*. It's also called a *revocable trust*. It lets the grantor stay in control of contributed assets while still alive.

A different kind of trust is an *irrevocable trust*. It puts the beneficiaries, not the grantor, in control of the contributed assets. It's most useful for lessening the size of an estate. That's because tax law sees assets contributed to an irrevocable trust as no longer belonging to the grantor. They're out of the estate, decreasing the bite that estate taxes can take.

Irrevocable trusts can have other benefits as well. For example, they may shield assets from legal judgments against a grantor. After all, the grantor no longer owns the assets.

But establishing an irrevocable trust is a very serious business. It's permanent. It can increase dependence. So for many families revocable trusts emerge as the more practical option.

Of course most people don't have trusts. Nor do they have ITF accounts, or beneficiaries. They'd think *payable on death* is a heavy metal band, and that *donees* are people who eat donuts. And no wonder. Estate planning is routinely wrapped in gobbledegook. It seems daunting. But much of it turns out to be easier than renewing a driver's license.

SUMMARY

1. Estate planning is arranging in advance where your assets will go once you've passed.
2. Good estate planning involves minimizing taxes and avoiding probate.
3. Taxes relevant to estate planning include estate taxes, gift taxes, and inheritance taxes.
4. Simple tools for avoiding probate include ITF accounts and trusts.

PART III

DO

CHAPTER 17

WORK

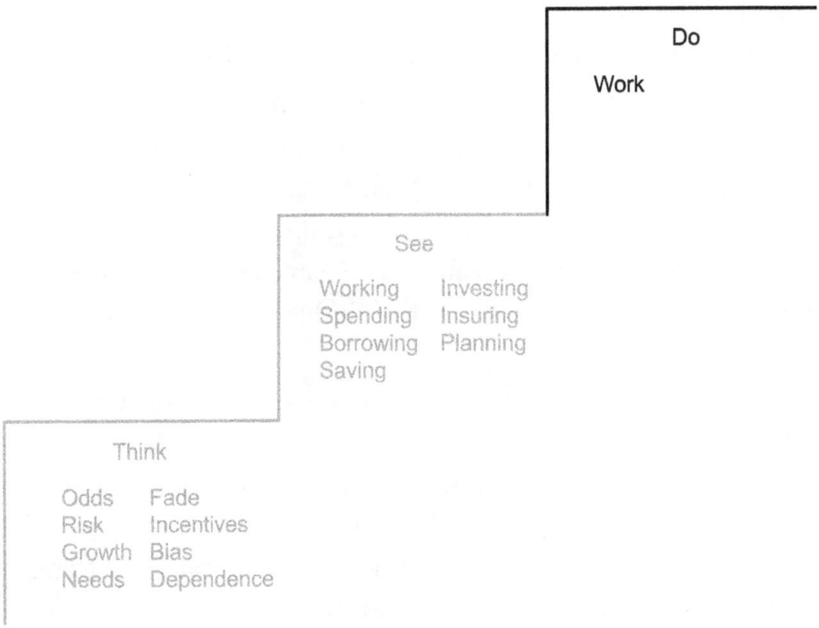

The seven spheres of personal finance are now clear. There's no fog. Working, spending, borrowing, saving, investing, insuring, and planning all appear plain. We view them as simple, because they are simple. It's straightforward, then, to know how best to approach each. Work, for starters.

You know that work isn't the main way to get rich, because of taxes. But it's still useful. To make it as useful as possible, make sure that it's *good work*. Good work has three hallmarks.

First, it interests you. It may interest you because it gives you the chance to perform needed services, learn new things, build new products, or just be part of an enterprise that you consider worthwhile.

Second, it puts you in the company of people that you admire. We naturally take on the characteristics of those that we associate with. Our colleagues plus time equals us. So choose a workplace filled with good influences. After all, you want to become someone that you like.

Third, it pays satisfactorily. Earned income may be taxed at a high rate. But it still lets you save, invest, and pay for needs.

No job is always dreamy. There will always be the occasional day that feels like a grind. But seek all three good characteristics and you can come pretty close to the ideal.

Bad work has the opposite three characteristics. It bores you, puts you in the company of bad influences, and doesn't pay enough. Avoid it.

If you find yourself in a bad work situation, find better opportunities. Find three, just as if you were getting three bids on a need. That way you'll really know what your options are.

If you only find one, keep looking. Find two more. If you find only two, search for a third. Seek three total because that creates for you real alternatives. It puts you in charge. Only with a good selection can you make a good choice.

Finding three is easier if the new opportunities come to you. With online professional networks like LinkedIn (in whose parent I am a shareholder), they can. Have your profile present you as the kind of person that you'd choose to work with. Set your preferences such that recruiters can contact you:

http://www.smallstepstorich.com/17.1.htm

Also, use *the strength of weak ties*. That's the power of the relationships you have with acquaintances.[1] Not friends, *acquaintances*. They're the people you know well enough to reach out to, but not so well that your social circle overlaps with theirs.

Acquaintances accelerate your job search because they know people that you don't, people with access to opportunities that you might not otherwise see. So let your acquaintances know that you're looking.

As you search, take care not to disrupt your current job situation. When you do leave your old employer, do so graciously. How you act while exiting is something that people will talk about, and the story they'll tell is one that you'll never have a chance to edit. Make it one that you'd hope they repeat often.

You can't predict exactly how leaving a good reputation will benefit you in the future. But the odds are that it will.

I remember my first visit to a Trader Joe's. It's a chain of grocery stores based in California. What struck me most was the employees. They stood out, somehow, from the people I'd seen working in other supermarkets.

At first it was hard to pin down exactly how they were different. But on my second or third visit, it became clear. They were *engaged*. Whether restocking shelves, sweeping floors, or bagging groceries, they were *into it*.

I've since learned that Trader Joe's has specific policies aimed at creating that culture. They pay more, delegate responsibility, and rotate assignments.[2] Such policies seem to inspire their people to lavish discretionary energy on their tasks. They buzz around with purpose. They get into a *flow*.

That's what good work feels like: a flow. It has a happy rhythm. I first saw it in a supermarket. But I've since seen it in all manner of companies. Make sure that it's in yours.

Once you have good work, make the most of the resources it provides.

When you need insurance, see if good deals are available through your employer, or through a family member's employer.

If your compensation includes stock options, be tax savvy with them. Remember that when you *exercise*—when you pay cash to own the stock—you'll owe tax if the market price is above the *strike price*. The strike price is the predetermined amount you pay to exercise. So make sure that you have enough cash to pay the tax, perhaps by selling the shares you receive right away.

In fact, it's probably wise not to exercise unless you're ready to sell the shares as soon as you get them. Your employer can help you manage this situation.

Provided that you have a sufficient cash buffer and no threatening debt, use advantaged accounts to the fullest. With a 401(k), contribute at least as much as your employer matches each year. In 2021 the most you could contribute was $19,500, or $26,000 if you were at least 50 years old. The same limits apply to 403(b) and 457 plans.[3]

With an IRA, contribute all the way up to the annual limit. The limit changes annually, varies with your income, and applies to traditional and Roth IRA contributions combined. For the 2021 tax year it tops out at $6,000, or $7,000 if you're at least 50 years old.[4]

What's better to contribute to, a Roth or a traditional? My personal opinion is that most people should first try to contribute as much as they can to a Roth. Here's why.

As we saw in chapter 10, Roth IRAs offer real advantages. You can withdraw contributions to them at any time without penalty. You're never required to take distributions, even when you're older. And if you do, you're not taxed on any of those distributions. That's a good deal.

The drawback, of course, is that contributions to a Roth IRA aren't tax deductible. But I would suggest that for many, giving up that tax deductibility isn't that expensive.

Think about it. Contributions to a traditional IRA are tax deductible only if your income is below a certain amount. The amount changes, but for 2021 it's basically $76,000.[5]

I say *basically* for two reasons, both of which are dreadfully boring.

One, the limit is technically $76,000 of *MAGI*. That's *modified adjusted gross income*. That's income minus select splurges like alimony; plus assorted curios like rental losses. Your tax return states your MAGI.

Two, the deduction actually phases out starting at $66,000 of MAGI. But for the moment let's assume that the deductibility disappears at an income of $76,000.

That level of income would put you in a relatively low tax bracket. For a single person it would be the third lowest, actually. There are four above it.

Now: how much is a tax deduction worth? That's easy math. It's the deduction times your tax rate.

Consider a $6,000 deduction. For the tax rate, you have a couple. There's your *tax bracket*, which you pay on the top tier of your income. Then there's your *effective tax rate*, a blend of the different rates you pay on the different tiers of your income. Fascinating, I know. But for now let's work with 25 percent. That would make the deduction worth $1,500. That's just $6,000 times 0.25.

If your income were higher, you'd be kicked up to a higher tax bracket. So the rate would be higher. Forty percent, say. In that case your $6,000 deduction would be worth $2,400. That's just $6,000 times 0.40. But if your MAGI was above $76,000, you couldn't take it.

And that's the point. Traditional IRA contribution deductions become most valuable *precisely when you can't take them*.

Of course if your cash buffer is too small and you have a low income year, perhaps you could really use that deduction. But then it might be best not to make any IRA contribution at all. It might be better to build your cash buffer back up to its healthy level.

Roth IRA contributions can only be made if your MAGI is below a certain ceiling. That ceiling resets often, but for the 2021 tax year it's $140,000 for a single person and $208,000 for someone married that files tax returns jointly.[6]

Above those levels you could still make contributions to a traditional IRA, but they wouldn't be tax deductible. Your MAGI would be too high. But it could still be wise to make them. This is for two reasons.

First, in the traditional IRA the contributions can grow *tax-deferred* for years. No taxes will be owed on any returns as long as they stay in there.

Second, you may be able to convert the traditional IRA into a Roth IRA. That's accomplished through a stunt called a *backdoor Roth IRA*. It's a nondeductible contribution to a traditional IRA that you then convert into a Roth IRA.

The rules governing backdoor Roth IRAs may change, so it's best to have your discount broker explain it. That's worth doing.

If you do make a non-deductible contribution to a traditional IRA, or do a backdoor Roth IRA conversion, you may need to file Form 8606 with the IRS.[7] It's usually generated as part of a normal annual tax return. Just make sure that it is.

You can make IRA contributions for a particular year either *during* that year, or in the first few months of the next year. You have until the tax return filing deadline—generally April 15—to make contributions for the prior year.[8]

The advantage to making contributions as early as possible is that they get a head start on their taxless march to greatness. Contribute on January 1 instead of April 15 the following year and you'll get over 15 months more of unbridled growth.

But most people might do better to wait until the following year. This is for two reasons.

First, it's only after the tax year has ended that you really know what your income was. That can determine if you're eligible to contribute at all, and if you are, what kind of IRA you should contribute to.

Second, you may owe a penalty if you make *excess contributions*. Avoid that by waiting until you know your MAGI.

Tax buccaneers may counter that early IRA contributions can be withdrawn without penalty under some circumstances. And they'd be right. But that can require you to file IRS Form 5329—enjoy!—and do some other somersaults as well.[9] Why bother?

If you switch employers, don't automatically cash in your old 401(k). That could trigger an unnecessary tax bill. Instead either keep it with your old employer, roll it over into a 401(k) at your new employer, or roll it over into an IRA.

Rolling it over to an IRA can make a lot of sense. It can spare you periodic 401(k) fees, and give you access to stock market index funds with lower expense ratios. The trick is to make sure that the rollover doesn't create any new costs, and doesn't trigger any tax liabilities. So make sure that it's a *direct rollover*.

A direct rollover keeps the change from looking like a withdrawal, which could trigger taxes and—depending on your age—penalties.[10] HR departments and financial institutions do direct rollovers all the time, so ask them for guidance.

If good work to you means starting a business, be realistic. Keep three somewhat contradictory truths in mind.

First, most startups fail. They may fail because they don't solve any particular problem for customers, or because they let fixed monthly expenses soar. They may fail because they depend on a single big supplier that hikes prices, or on a single big client that stops ordering. Whatever the cause, most startups ultimately run out of cash and shut down.

That's discouraging, of course. Plus, it's hard to believe. After all, the selection bias shows us more successes than failures. Dead companies don't put out press releases. Flops hide.

But successes sparkle. They get the attention of bloggers, journalists, and influencers. That's why we know about them. So correctly see them as outliers, not averages.

Second, cultural attitudes towards entrepreneurship vary around the world. In Silicon Valley, it's revered. Even the flops get props. But in some other places new venture failures are reviled. That can make it hard to bounce back. So consider how entrepreneurship is perceived in your community.

Third, successful entrepreneurs stay positive. Not pollyannaish, but positive. Their optimism serves them well by radiating an infectious zeal to customers, suppliers, and employees. Those other parties respond favorably, mirroring the entrepreneur's glow.

Entrepreneurs in the U.S. have access to some resources that other folks don't. *SEP IRAs*, for example. SEP stands for *simplified employee pension*. It's like a traditional IRA, with two big differences.

First, contributions to it are made by the business, not by the entrepreneur. The contributions are tax-deductible expenses for the business, and aren't taxable to the entrepreneur when made. That's a good deal.

Second, the annual contribution limits are higher. For the 2021 tax year the limit is 25 percent of compensation or $58,000, whichever is lower.[11]

SEP IRAs make the most sense for businesses with a tiny number of employees. One, for example. That's largely because the annual contributions need to be the same percentage of compensation for every employee.

There are some wrinkles to SEP IRAs. You can only have one if you're at least age 21, and have worked for the business for at least three of the last five years.[12] But they're worth tackling. SEP IRA accounts are offered through discount brokerages, who can explain their current benefits and conditions.

Work occupies your most alert hours. So get it right. Since it's not the main route to wealth, make sure to use the advantaged account opportunities that it provides. And be certain that it interests you and leads you towards becoming the kind of person that you want to be. Insist that it get you into a flow. Should you forget what that looks like, visit my supermarket.

SUMMARY

1. Do work that interests you, puts you in the company of good influences, and pays satisfactorily.
2. If your work does not interest you, puts you in the company of bad influences, or pays unsatisfactorily, find three different opportunities.
3. If you have a cash buffer and no threatening debt, contribute to your 401(k) or 403(b) at least as much as your employer will match each year.
4. If you have a cash buffer and no threatening debt, also maximize annual contributions to other advantaged accounts like IRAs.
5. When exercising stock options at a gain, make sure you wind up with enough cash to pay the resulting tax liability.
6. If you switch employers, don't automatically cash in your old 401(k).
7. Most startups fail. Those that succeed do so in part because their founders stay positive.

CHAPTER 18

SELECT

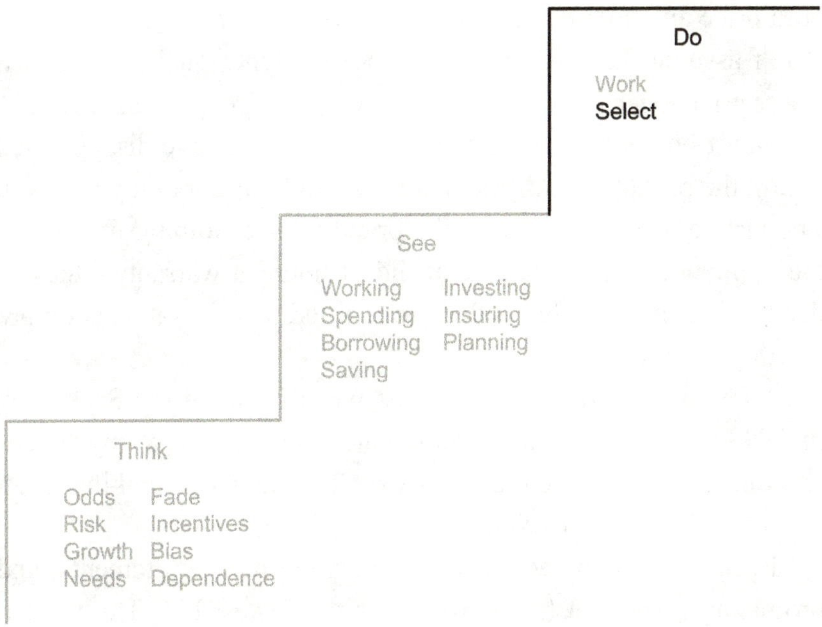

Don't just spend. *Select*. Be *selective*.

When you select, you spend on purpose. You meet all needs, fully and well; and rightly ignore mere wants.

Use three tools to ensure that you're being selective: pauses, bids, and budgets.

First are pauses. Delay before buying anything. Delay to neutralize the snap instincts that dress up mere wants as needs. Waiting lets such imposters fade away.

Have a pause policy. It can be based on money, or on products. Both can work. A money-based pause policy has you holding any cash you earn for a day, a week, or a month—you choose the period—before spending it. A product-based pause policy has you waiting for a day, a week, or a month before making any contemplated buy.

Second is bids. Get three bids before buying anything. Consider different vendors for any significant purchase. Weigh both price and quality. And regard those as distinct considerations. Don't assume that a higher price means higher quality, or that a lower price means lower quality. Let each factor speak for itself.

Don't bother getting bids from vendors that have disappointed you in the past. The odds are that they would disappoint you again. The airline that bumped you, the brand whose clothing unraveled, the appliance manufacturer that didn't honor a warranty—they're dead to you now. Only vendors committed to your satisfaction are worth your time.

Three bids works. I learned this when I bought my Saab back in 1998. I found the three Saab dealerships closest to my house, and did enough research to know exactly what I was looking for: a black 900S turbo coup with no options.

I sent a letter to each dealership stating my requirements, and promising to pay cash that week for the lowest bid. The written offer I accepted was a full 6 percent below the second lowest. That was quite a savings. Plus I avoided the showroom haggling that can make new car buying unpleasant.

Third is budgets. Have a budget that's both income-based and zero-based.

On the income side, spend less each month than your take-home pay. Keep track by using spreadsheets, or a budgeting site:

http://www.smallstepstorich.com/18.1.htm

On the zero side, make every product that wants to come work for you interview for the position. Have it prove to you that it has utility. If it doesn't, don't hire it.

Budgeting applies a bit differently to buying a home. That's because it usually concerns monthly payments, not the total purchase price. After all, most home purchases are financed with mortgages. That spreads the cost out over years.

Homebuying should still be regarded as selecting, however. Whatever its investment merits may be, a primary residence is firstly meant to be consumed. Its market price may rise over time, but the odds are that it will do so only at the rate of inflation.

You should still make full use of a home's investment incentives, of course. For example, we saw how when you sell your home at a gain, part of that gain is tax-free. Since 1997 that part could reach $250,000, or $500,000 for a married couple that files their tax return jointly.[1]

Plus the basis used for calculating that gain may be higher than what you originally paid for the home. That's good. It can, for example, include *closing costs* like transfer taxes and utility service installation charges. It can also include improvements, like the addition of a deck or a garage.

IRS publication 523 has not, to my knowledge, won any literary prizes. But it does guide you through the pleasure of increasing your basis:

http://www.smallstepstorich.com/18.2.htm

Another investment merit of a home is that you can rent it out for up to 14 days per year tax-free.[2] That's a bonus. But again, it's not enough to move home buying out of the realm of selecting.

If you rent your home, you may periodically think about buying. We've seen how that decision belongs in the context of selecting, not investing. It could be reasonably driven by wanting some stability for a family, for example.

Nonetheless, a *rent vs. buy analysis* may be useful. It looks at numbers alone. If you're on the fence, it can bring some clarity.

Some of the factors that go into a rent vs. buy analysis are knowable. They include your monthly rent, the price of the home you'd buy, and how much of a down payment you'd make.

But other factors are harder to nail down. They include how long you'd own the home, how much the home's price will appreciate, and future tax rates.

Despite these uncertainties, several online tools take a stab at the rent vs. buy decision. The best ones are worth trying, if only to better understand which factors most impact the choice. For example:

http://www.smallstepstorich.com/18.3.htm

If you need a home somewhere for a discrete period of time, lease. It may be easier than purchasing. After all, bookending some temporary out-of-town gig with the hullabaloo of buying and selling property may be too much.

Leasing may also make sense if you live in a high-cost area. If you're in coastal California, New York City, or other place with astronomical home prices, a rent vs. buy analysis may come out in favor of renting.

But as a rule, don't lease. Don't regard it as a sensible way to secure the use of something, particularly if that something is a car. Leasing may roll off the tongue of a salesperson as if it were the most natural option on earth, every bit as sound as buying. But it's not. As we saw in chapter 11, it's often a deceptively expensive ruse that leaves you with nothing.

Incidentally, the words *lease* and *rent* mean basically the same thing. The only difference is time. Leases tend to be for longer periods than rental agreements.

One sort of spending that no one really selects but that is nonetheless unavoidable is income taxes. It too can be streamlined. Whether you work with a tax preparer or an online service, file returns early, and pay any amounts owed fully. There's no benefit to procrastinating. Filing and paying next month will be neither easier nor cheaper. It will, however, be more stressful.

If you engage a tax preparer that doesn't share your quest for promptness, gently dismiss that person. Interview three potential replacements, and pick one.

In fact, fire *anything* that doesn't work for you.

If you're charged monthly for a service that you don't use and there's no termination fee, cancel it. If you pay for more of a service than you need, ratchet the subscription down to a lower level. If you connect to the internet through your cable television service but don't watch the premium channels, cancel the premium channels. If your mobile phone carrier charges you for more talk, text, and data than you could ever possibly use, switch to a more basic tier of service.

Same with goods. If you own things that no longer have utility for you, sell them. If you store those things in a rented storage facility, cancel the rental once they're gone.

Selling used goods is simple. List them for free on sites like Craigslist or Facebook Marketplace. Other countries have similar sites, like Kijiji in Canada and Gumtree in the UK and Australia. When you write your listing, ask respondents to include a phone number in their reply. That nicely screens out folks that aren't really interested.

I've made great use of such sites. I've used Craigslist to sell a glass credenza, a box spring, and a dining room table whose top I'd once refinished so inexpertly it looked lunar.

That's the miracle of online classifieds. They make things you no longer need walk out on their own. They're like junk hauling services that pay *you*.

If debt has been a recurring problem, pay for products only with cash or—as long as it doesn't come with an overdraft line of credit—a debit card.

Otherwise, pay bills immediately. With vendors you trust, do this by setting up automatic bill pay. Or pay manually using the online bill pay function of your CMA (cash management account), MMA (money market account), or traditional bank account.

Allow no time to pass between receiving and paying a bill. This eliminates a whole raft of complications. Most obviously, it makes late fees and interest charges impossible. It also lessens the worry that comes from forgetting what's been paid and what hasn't.

Being selective is different from being *stingy*. To be stingy is to not fulfill needs. It's volunteering to yearn for essentials. There's no merit to it.

But there's great merit to being selective. And that merit shows up right away. That's because what isn't spent is instantly saved. Of course that by itself won't make you rich. But it's part of an overall approach that will.

SUMMARY

1. Select. Spend only on purpose.
2. Use pauses, bids, and budgets to ensure that you're being selective.
3. Regard buying a home as selecting, not investing.
4. Lease only in particular circumstances.
5. File tax returns early and pay any amounts owed fully.
6. Cancel unused subscriptions, and ratchet down underused subscriptions.
7. Sell any goods that have lost their utility.
8. Pay bills immediately, either automatically or by receiving and paying them in the same sitting.
9. Being selective has merit, but being stingy does not.

CHAPTER 19

UNBORROW

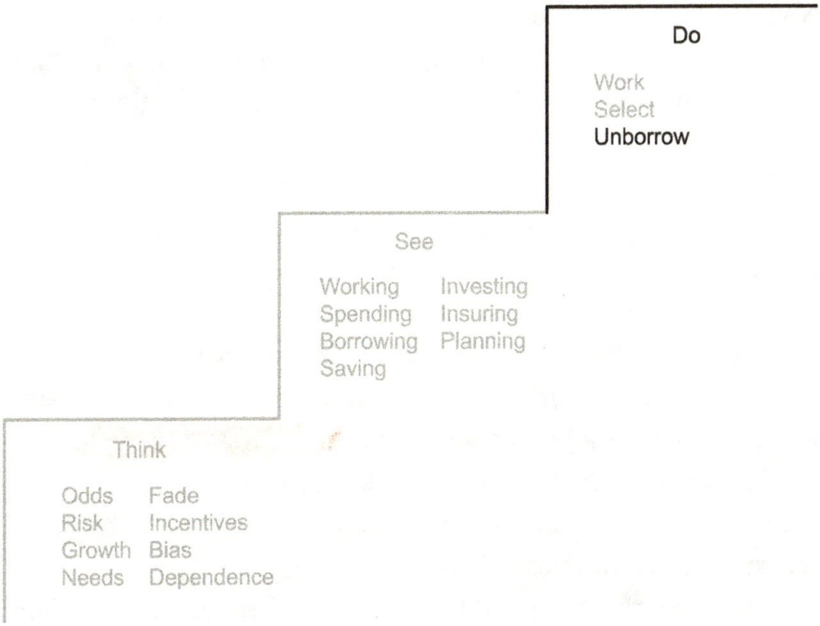

Don't borrow money. Instead, *unborrow*.

Unborrowing is the double drill of paying down debt and not taking on new debt. It's almost always the right thing to do. That's because most borrowing increases risk a lot. It's *threatening debt*.

To be sure, there are exceptions. We've seen debt that's *not-so-threatening*. It charges little interest, and is used to buy a primary residence or—under some circumstances—an education. We'll get to those.

But as a default guideline, unborrow.

If you have threatening debt, fear not. There are straightforward ways to pay it down. We'll get to those too. But first let's clarify why paying down debt makes so much sense.

Paying down debt returns well. Monstrously well. It returns better than actual investing.

Consider a debt with an annual interest rate of 15 percent. An outstanding balance on a credit card, for example. Paying it off would, obviously, make the 15 percent expense go away.

That's a 15 percent annual return. Compare that to the 7 percent return from a low-cost stock index fund. It's not even close.

Plus, the return from paying down debt is guaranteed. There's zero uncertainty. The odds of getting it are 100 percent. And it comes immediately. There's none of this waiting around for decades rigmarole.

For that reason, don't invest before paying down any threatening debt. Don't contribute to an IRA, or put any money into a taxable stock brokerage account. Repay the debt first.

To do that faster, scale back spending. Tighten up the definition of needs. Be even more selective. After all, 15 percent return opportunities don't show up every day.

Many people have multiple debts. They may have a home equity line of credit, a student loan, and an outstanding credit card balance. Which should they pay down first?

One option is to start with the debt that has the highest interest rate. After all, that's the most expensive. Repaying it first would deliver the biggest return sooner.

Or, start with the smallest debt. That's the one with the lowest balance. That would quickly make one of the burdens disappear entirely.

I personally like the first approach. It appeals to my inner mathematician.

But the second is okay too. It offers the satisfaction of erasing an obligation completely. It's a speedy victory that says *you can do this*. To someone having trouble starting a debt reduction program, it's motivating.

Which approach one picks isn't as important as just picking one. *Now*. Because what can not work is the popular route of picking neither.

Understandably, it can take time to pay off multiple debts. So if you have credit card debt, call the issuer and ask for a lower interest rate. Just pick up the phone. Say that you've been offered a great rate by a competitor—card issuers send out so many offers that that's certainly true—and are thinking about transferring your balance. But you first want to give them a chance to keep your business. If you're feeling plucky, don't hang up until they give you a lower rate. Make them end the call first.

Avoid the temptation to transfer outstanding balances to a new card with a low teaser rate. After all, teaser rates end. Plus, getting a new card just sustains the threatening debt habit. One doesn't want to get good at reckless borrowing. It's not a skill to be mastered. It's a weakness to be squashed.

Credit card companies are expert at encouraging our bad behavior. Just look at your most recent statement. Prominently displayed is the *minimum payment* amount. Pay just that and you'll get hit with an interest expense. So ignore that minimum. It's for suckers. You want to pay the entire balance. Always.

When you regularly pay the entire balance, credit cards become useful. That's because of their perks. Many offer reward points, for example. I've used one airline's Visa card for years, and haven't paid for domestic air travel in a decade. Others offer cash back. Still others provide the collision and comprehensive part of car rental insurance.

But just one underpayment can eclipse such plusses. Points, cash back, and other bonuses drown in a sea of late fees and interest.

Don't use debt consolidators or debt counselors. Too often they're expensive, deceitful, or both.

While most debt is threatening, not all is. For that reason it's useful to maintain the option of borrowing on favorable terms. So stay creditworthy. That means having a good *credit report* and a high *credit score*.

A credit report is a summary of your debt and bill payment history. It's tracked by three nationwide agencies: Equifax, Experian, and TransUnion.

Federal law gives you the right to check your credit report with each agency annually, for free. That's worth doing, in part because you can have any errors corrected:

http://www.smallstepstorich.com/19.1.htm

If you're about to apply for a loan, it's fine to check all three at once. If not, perhaps it's better to spread them out. Maybe Equifax in January, Experian in May, and TransUnion in September, for example. That way you can monitor any month-to-month inaccuracies that pop up.

Some of those inaccuracies can be amusing. I once checked my credit report and found that one of the agencies thought I worked for an outfit called Eureka Trucking. The error was easily fixed. I just phoned the agency, and it promptly made the correction. But I must admit that this all had me pondering what might have been, my forsaken life on the open road.

A credit score is a number between 300 and 850. It's also called a *FICO score* after Fair Isaac Corporation, the company that originated it. The higher your credit score, the better.

Your credit score is generally not on your credit report. But it may be available for free through your bank, brokerage, or credit card company. Log in to your accounts and see. Failing that, purchase it directly from Fair Isaac:

http://www.smallstepstorich.com/19.2.htm

Three practices help you to maintain a good credit report and a high credit score.

First, pay all debts and bills on time and in full. That's a good idea anyway, of course. And it's easy to do if you've set your bills up for automatic payment, as noted earlier.

Second, have unused borrowing capacity. Your credit card company allows you to have an outstanding balance up to some limit. Having unused borrowing capacity means staying well under that limit.

Third, apply for credit only rarely. Limit the number of times you sign up for a loan, home rental, utility, or mobile phone service. Such applications trigger a *hard credit inquiry*. It's also called a *hard pull*. It temporarily notches down your credit score.

So can asking your credit card company for a lower interest rate, incidentally. But if you're in the process of paying off debt, that may be a hard pull worth taking.

When you check your own credit report or credit score, that triggers only a *soft credit inquiry*. It's also called a *soft pull*. It doesn't impact your credit score.[1]

We've seen how one type of not-so-threatening debt is a conforming mortgage on a primary residence. That's partly because housing is a need. Plus *conforming* means that the interest rate will be low relative to *nonconforming*—which basically means bigger—mortgages.

Get at least three bids on a mortgage. Each must be from a completely different source. Three bids from one mortgage broker counts as just one, as does three bids from one mortgage comparison website.

When a mortgage lender checks your credit, it will probably trigger a hard pull. It may temporarily tick your credit score down a bit. But when additional mortgage lenders also check your credit, no additional hard pulls are triggered provided that those inquiries happen during the same period. The length of that period varies, but is no longer than 45 days.[2] So get all of your bids within the same week or two.

If you are or were in the U.S. military, or are the surviving spouse of someone who was, first look into a VA-backed mortgage:

http://www.smallstepstorich.com/19.3.htm

Otherwise, find the lenders most likely to offer attractive rates with a comparison site:

http://www.smallstepstorich.com/19.4.htm

In your research you'll learn more about exactly what characteristics you want your mortgage to have. There are four key choices to make.

The first is the *down payment.* That's the percentage of the home's price you'll pay for with your own cash. The rest will be financed with the mortgage. Avoid complications by making your down payment at least 20 percent of the home's purchase price.

Second is term. Most mortgages last for either 15 or 30 years. Fifteen year mortgages tend to have lower interest rates, and are less expensive overall. But 30 year mortgages have lower monthly payments. They're more common.

Third is whether the interest rate should be fixed or floating.

A fixed-rate mortgage features the same payment every month. Part of each payment goes towards interest, and part goes towards principal. Early on, most of each payment goes towards interest. That's because the principal is still big, and the interest rate times a big number equals a lot of interest. Over time more of each payment goes towards principal.

An online *amortization schedule* calculator can show the split between interest and principal each month:

http://www.smallstepstorich.com/19.5.htm

An *adjustable-rate mortgage*—or *ARM*—is different. Its rate is fixed for an initial number of years. Then it can float within a specified range.

An ARM's name describes some of its characteristics. It says how long the rate is fixed, and how frequently it can reset thereafter.

For example, a *5/2 ARM* has a fixed interest rate for the first five years, and then a floating rate that can reset every two years. A *10/1 ARM* has a fixed rate for the first decade, and then a floating rate that can reset annually.

The initial fixed rate on an ARM is often lower than the rate on a fixed rate mortgage of the same term. So ARMs tend to make more sense for homebuyers that are sure they'll sell the home before the fixed rate period ends.

Fourth regards *points*. That's real estate slang for *discount points*. They let you pay extra money at the inception of a mortgage in exchange for a lower interest rate.

A point generally costs 1 percent of the starting amount of the mortgage. Each point usually reduces the interest rate by 0.25 percent.

For example, consider a $500,000, 30 year, 4 percent fixed rate mortgage. One point would cost $5,000. That's just 1 percent of $500,000.

That point would bring the annual interest rate down to 3.75 percent. That's just 4 percent minus 0.25 percent.

It makes more sense to buy points the longer you own the home. The traditional way to see this is through the *payback period*. That's how long it takes to recoup the upfront cost.

In our example, the upfront cost is $5,000. See how long it would take to recoup that amount with an online calculator:

http://www.smallstepstorich.com/19.6.htm

In this case the payback period seems to be 70 months. That's almost six years. So the online calculator recommends buying a point if you plan on keeping the home for at least that long.

But that reasoning has a flaw. It fails to consider *opportunity cost*. That's what you could have done with the $5,000 instead of buying the point.

For example, you could have put the $5,000 in a high-yield online savings account. Granted, in 2022 that may return less than 1 percent. But at least it's something.

Or you could have increased your down payment. By taking out a mortgage for only $495,000, your $5,000 would effectively earn a return equal to the mortgage's interest rate. That's 4 percent. That's better.

I personally like the second option. The return is higher. Plus, why borrow what you don't need?

In addition, consider the complexities of the points system. It could have been set up more plainly. But it wasn't. The odds are slim that financial institutions obfuscated a mortgage feature that actually helps you.

Points are regarded as prepaid interest for tax purposes. So they're tax deductible.[3] That's good. But it's still not enough to win me over.

We know that mortgages carry interest costs. But they also have *closing costs*. That's the sum of payments made at the start of the loan. It includes any discount points. It also includes expenses like an *origination fee*, which is paid to the mortgage lender.

Closing costs are always negotiable. Sometimes the mortgage lender—or the seller of the home—can be persuaded to pay for some of them. Ask. Better yet, gently insist.

Try to find a mortgage with no prepayment penalty. That way you'll avoid an extra expense if you find yourself in the fortunate position of being able to pay your mortgage off early.

Mortgages last for a long time. During that period, interest rates can drop. If they do, it can make sense to *refinance*. That's taking out a new mortgage to replace an old one, generally to secure a lower interest rate and lower monthly payments.

A refinanced mortgage has closing costs too. So a basic way to see if refinancing makes sense is through payback period analysis. Just see how long it would take to recoup the closing costs through the reduction in monthly payments, and make sure that you plan on owning the home for at least that long. There are online calculators for that too:

http://www.smallstepstorich.com/19.7.htm

As with points calculators, refinance calculators fail to consider opportunity cost. After all, refinance closing costs could have been used to pay down more of the mortgage.

But refinance calculators have an even bigger problem. They downplay how refinancing can extend your total mortgage term.

To illustrate, assume that you took out a 30 year fixed rate mortgage 15 years ago. Since then, interest rates have plummeted. So you consider refinancing. That could lower your monthly payments. But if the new mortgage is for 30 years, that would push out the date on which you become mortgage-free by a decade and a half. By the end you would have paid interest for a total of 45 years.

A better choice might be to refinance with a 15 year mortgage. If that meant a lower monthly payment and quickly-recouped closing costs, your expenses would go down without extending your total mortgage term.

Even better would be making your total mortgage term shorter. If you could refinance with a 10 year mortgage that had a lower fixed interest rate, lower monthly payments, and quickly-recouped closing costs, you'd win many times over. That's a pretty rare situation, but it nicely illustrates an ideal.

Another kind of not-so-threatening debt is a student loan for college or graduate school. Education could certainly be considered a need. Plus there are ways to minimize the loan's interest rate. But a student loan should only be pursued after three other options are exhausted.

Scholarships, for one. They're offered by governments, universities, corporations, foundations, and clubs. They're generally merit-based, aimed at students with above-average talent in sports or academics. They offer free money, so it's worth spending many hours pursuing them.

Another is grants. They're given by the same kinds of organizations that offer scholarships. They're free money too. But they're generally needs-based, targeted at students that would otherwise have a difficult time paying for school. Again, it's worthwhile to dedicate significant time applying for them.

A third option is a less expensive school. Private colleges are costly. But many states have outstanding public universities that charge much less. In some countries they're free. Choosing such an institution could erase the need for a loan entirely.

Only after scholarships, grants, and public schools have been explored should a student loan be considered. Get at least three bids, of course. And start with federal sources, since they often offer the lowest interest rates:

http://www.smallstepstorich.com/19.8.htm

Make sure that the school that will get your borrowed money delivers not just a good education, but a brand name education. It must be well known. It has to be highly regarded in the places you'd consider living, and in the industries in which you'd consider working.

For many years I've taught at Stanford and Berkeley. Both offer a good education. But many schools offer a good education. What sets Stanford and Berkeley apart, in my view, is that they're both highly regarded. Their graduates look accomplished to potential employers all over the world.

I hate debt. But those schools—and others like them—have reputations that may actually be worth borrowing for.

There's a good argument for keeping not-so-threatening debt outstanding even once you're in a position to pay it down. It's based on the gap between the interest rate and investment returns.

For example, say that you have a conforming mortgage with a 4 percent fixed interest rate. As you know, a low-cost stock index fund returns an after-tax annual average of around 7 percent.

Assume that you have cash in excess of many years worth of your expenses. You could use your excess savings to pay down the entire mortgage. That would return 4 percent.

Or you could invest it in the fund. Then you'd basically be borrowing at 4 percent to make 7 percent. Mathematically, that's a win. It's like having a low interest rate margin account without having to pledge the investments as collateral.

The same logic can be used by homebuyers rich enough to not even need a mortgage. They may still take out conforming mortgages because the interest rate is below the average after-tax return on a low-cost stock index fund.

Many people like these tactics, and understandably so. But I personally don't care for them. Freedom from debt strikes me as more attractive.

That's the thing about borrowing. It's the antithesis of freedom. It comes with required payments to make, ascending rate indexes to fear, and cryptic loan documents to decipher. Who needs that, especially if one literally doesn't need that?

SUMMARY

1. Unborrow. Pay down debt and don't take on new debt.
2. Paying down debt often returns better than actual investing.
3. Don't invest before paying down all threatening debt.
4. Accelerate paying down debt by being more selective.
5. Skip debt consolidators, debt counselors, and balance transfers to new credit cards.
6. Pay credit card balances in full every month.
7. Stay creditworthy so that not-so-threatening debt is available to you.
8. Get at least three bids on any borrowing.
9. Scholarships, grants, and great schools that cost less beat student loans.

CHAPTER 20

SAVE

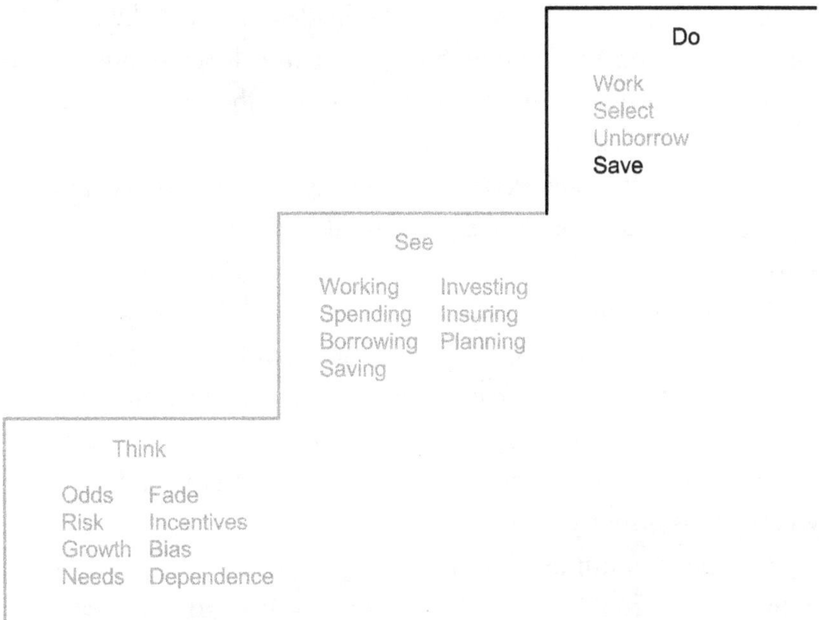

Save earned cash.

You'll feel the benefits immediately. You'll have confidence, and justifiably so. That's because you'll know that you can pay for needs. You'll be insulated. Concerns over money will lighten.

Also, you'll have the raw material necessary to invest. You'll have cash to commit to higher-returning opportunities.

At a minimum, save a quarter of a year's worth of expenses. That's your starting cash buffer.

Begin by revisiting your annual expenses. We calculated that back in chapter 1.

Your expenses may change over time, of course. They may go down as you unmask mere wants posing as needs. Or they may go up, if your needs grow. Nailing it down precisely isn't critical. But getting it approximately correct is. So occasionally reassess it. If your costs change, adjust your buffer.

I appreciate that at certain stages of life saving isn't easy. Needs may be great, income may be inadequate, and the economy may be bad. But I also know how powerful it feels to have at least a quarter of a year's worth of expenses in the bank. It brings a calm that you deserve. Please pursue it.

After you've secured your starting cash buffer, pay off threatening debt. Don't save more until you do. Once that's done, start saving more.

But how much?

The common answer to this question involves some percent of take-home pay. *Save 20 percent of your income*, for example. That's well-intentioned guidance. But in my view, it's backwards. It's backwards because how much you should save is a function of your expenses, not your income.

So save a multiple of your expenses. Think annual. You started with a multiple of one-fourth. As your means grow, increase that multiple. Perhaps the next milestone is one-half, then three-fourths, then one.

As noted earlier, my multiple is three. Admittedly, that's probably excessive. I pay dearly for it in the form of foregone investment returns. But it erases much concern, which I like. I happily spend to consume a product called tranquility.

As your wealth grows, so does the amount you could keep in cash. So it's useful to pick a maximum multiple. Under normal circumstances, it seems hard to justify anything higher than four. One could reasonably add amounts for upcoming costs like a down payment on a home. But beyond that, one drifts into oversaving. And since that's the same thing as underinvesting, it's not helpful.

It's fine to start your savings in a traditional bank account. But as noted earlier, a CMA (cash management account) or an MMA (money management account) may be better. Consider ones from three different discount brokerages. Make sure that they're all government insured, pay interest, charge no fees, have online bill pay, and can receive direct deposits.

Once you pick one, close your traditional bank account. You'll no longer need it.

As your savings pile up, open a high-yield online savings account. It too must be government insured, and can't have any fees. Consider three, using a comparison site:

http://www.smallstepstorich.com/20.1.htm

Then select the one that seems easiest to use and offers the highest rate. Link it to your traditional bank account, CMA, or MMA.

Use automated savings plans. They're just too easy to ignore. Have some amount of the salary that arrives in your traditional bank account, CMA, or MMA shot directly into your high-yield online savings account.

If you choose to keep a high multiple of your expenses in cash, you'll eventually approach the FDIC-insured limit in your high-yield account. In that case, open another.

Before you do, make sure that the new account is truly separate from other banks you already use. To illustrate, consider EmigrantDirect. It's an online identity of Emigrant Bank. But so are DollarSavingsDirect and MySavingsDirect. All three are part of the same outfit. So someone with $250,000 saved at EmigrantDirect, $250,000 at DollarSavingsDirect, and $250,000 at MySavingsDirect would only be covered up to $250,000 in total.[1] Don't be that person.

Never exceed the FDIC-insured limit at any single bank. It doesn't matter how stable the institution looks, or how strong the economy seems. Increasing risk for nothing is pointless.

Clever couples can boost the FDIC-insured limit up to $1,000,000. It's simple. Just open one account in one partner's name, another account in the other partner's name, and a third account held jointly. The first two will each be insured to $250,000, and the third will be insured to $500,000.[2] Any competent bank offering high-yield online savings accounts can guide you through this process.

As noted earlier, most banks offer CDs with fixed rates of interest that exceed the floating rates of their liquid accounts. They tempt. But early withdrawal penalties can easily wipe out the bonus interest. That's why I don't use them.

I must confess, however, that I once did. I was 14. I had some savings, and interest rates were high. So I compared CDs from three different banks near our house in Irvine, California. The lucky winner was World Savings on Michelson Drive. I whooshed down there on my 10-speed bike and wrote a check to buy a 90-day CD.

Three months later—no unexpected costs having soured my juvenile life—I biked back and *rolled it over*, meaning bought another one. There must be security camera footage of this somewhere.

I repeated this drill throughout junior high school. Eventually rates dropped, and I discovered stocks.

It's not skateboarding or video games for which I'm nostalgic. It's rollovers.

If you're saving beyond your normal cash buffer in anticipation of a major expense—like a down payment on a home—it may make sense to use CDs. But only if the rate is materially higher, and only if you're certain that the down payment won't be needed before the CD matures.

Even then disappointments can arise. The interest rate on a CD may look high compared to a liquid high-yield online savings account. But the CD rate is fixed, while the account rate floats. The latter could rise while your down payment is stuck in the CD.

If your savings start to approach real scale—millions—it may make sense to buy Treasurys directly from the U.S. government. This is for two reasons. First, an individual holding millions in high-yield online savings accounts would have to manage tens of different accounts to stay under the government-insured limit. That's doable, but bothersome.

Second, interest earned on Treasurys is tax-free at the state and local level.[3]

Technically, Treasurys aren't cash. They're fixed income securities. But they're backed by Uncle Sam, the same dude that's behind FDIC insurance. Plus they're traded so continuously that they're considered *cash-equivalent*. That means that they're readily convertible into cash without penalty.

Treasurys are easy to buy online:

http://www.smallstepstorich.com/20.2.htm

If you use a financial advisor, you may be encouraged to park some of your savings in investment grade corporate or municipal bonds. Those too are fixed income securities.

Such advice is well intentioned. But while Treasurys are cash equivalent, corporate and municipal bonds aren't. That's because sometimes—rarely, but sometimes—they're hard to sell for full value. Even bonds issued by blue chip companies can be hard to convert into cash during periods of extreme market turmoil.

Bonds aren't meritless. They may be useful to you in retirement. When earnings from work stop, investment grade bond funds can provide income used to pay for needs. Buying bonds is less about saving and more about investing, so we'll cover this topic in the next chapter.

If the country you live in has a stable currency, save in that currency. If you live in the U.S., save in dollars. If you live half time in the U.S. and half time in England, save half in U.S. dollars and half in British pounds. Denominate your savings in the currency of your expenses to avoid drifting into the low-return arena of foreign exchange.

But perhaps not if a country you spend time in has a currency that's unstable. Maybe the country has a high rate of inflation, for example. Or perhaps it has *exchange controls* that limit what you can do with its currency. In that case it may make sense to keep your savings in America, and to cover expenses in the other country by exchanging money when necessary.

If you have savings in one country but expenses in another, you may need to periodically transfer cash internationally. That's done easily and inexpensively with an online money transfer service. The best ones quote the fair *mid-market rate*, and disclose their fees upfront. For example:

http://www.smallstepstorich.com/20.3.htm

If you have financial accounts in multiple countries, stay aware of any special reporting laws. For example, Americans with non-U.S. accounts may be required to file an *FBAR*. That's the curiously out-of-order acronym for *Report of Foreign Bank and Financial Accounts*. It's an annual online filing that's easy and free. Fun, almost:

http://www.smallstepstorich.com/20.4.htm

Form 8938, or *Statement of Specified Foreign Financial Assets*, may also be required.[4] It too is straightforward. It's usually generated as part of a tax return.

Saving is simple to get right. It's about having enough cash, but not too much; and warehousing it in sensible places. By itself, it doesn't make you rich. But as we'll see in the next chapter, it sets the stage for the investing that does.

SUMMARY

1. Save cash to decrease worry and facilitate investing.
2. Your proper level of savings is a multiple of your expenses.
3. Reassess your average expenses as your needs change.
4. Save a cash buffer of at least a quarter of a year's worth of expenses.
5. Don't save more than a quarter of a year's worth of expenses until threatening debt is paid off.
6. Consider using a CMA or MMA instead of a traditional bank account.
7. Save most of your cash in high-yield online savings accounts, or at real scale, maybe in Treasurys.
8. Never keep more than the government-insured limit in any single bank.
9. Save in the currency of your expenses, assuming that currency is stable.
10. Don't save so much that you're underinvesting.

CHAPTER 21

INVEST

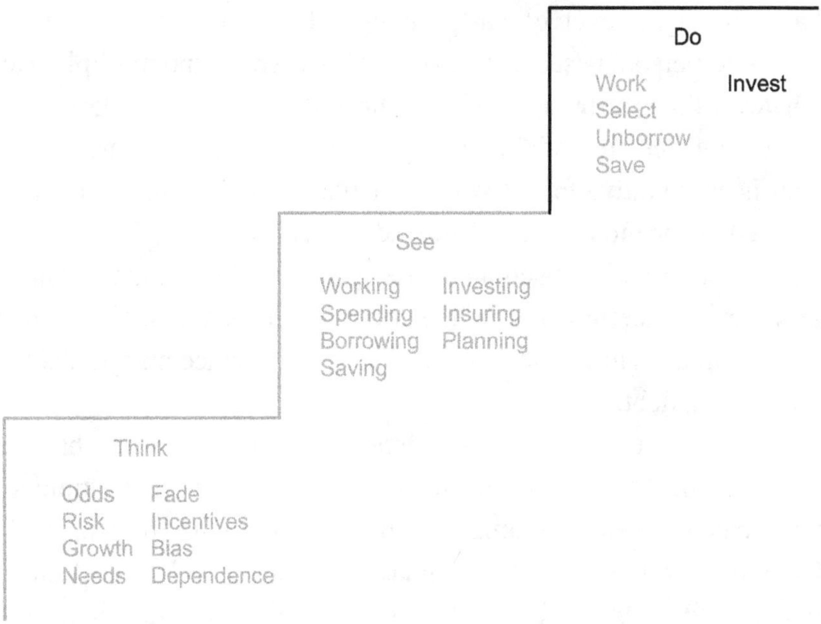

Invest with the odds. The odds say three things.

First, listed stocks return best. Over time, public shares beat other asset classes.

Second, passive beats active. No matter how clever or well-intentioned stock pickers are, they're routinely steamrolled by basic equity indexes.

Third, stock prices are unpredictable in the short term. We know that they'll go up in aggregate over decades. But we have no idea what they'll do tomorrow, next month, or even next year.

Invest also knowing that fees clip growth viciously. We've seen how an annual charge of only 1 percent can leave you with just three-quarters of the wealth that you deserve.

These understandings of odds and growth all boil down to a tidy marching order: make regular investments in low-cost stock index funds.

Before you do, remember to have two things in place. First, have the right level of cash savings. That amount varies from person to person, based as it is on one's expenses and multiple. But whatever the proper cash buffer is, have it.

Second, be free of threatening debt. Paying down threatening debt is so lucrative that if you still have any left you should savor this last chance to earn such stupendous returns.

Invest through a discount brokerage. Consider accounts from at least three different firms. When you pick one, set things up so that buying on margin is impossible. That's smart, since margin debt is threatening debt.

Invest first with your advantaged accounts. If you have a 401(k), contribute at least as much to it each year as your employer will match. Then, maximize annual contributions to your IRA. Commit amounts in your advantaged accounts to low-cost stock index funds. Only after that's done should you start investing through a taxable brokerage account.

Make your investments regularly. On the same date of each month, for example. Such a schedule keeps biases from tampering with your good financial habits.

Regular investments can be made automatically, or manually.

To make them automatically, set up an automatic investment plan with your brokerage. Have it shoot a portion of your take-home pay into a low-cost index fund. You'll likely be limited to using mutual funds. Those lack the tax efficiency of ETFs. But an automatic plan gives you one less monthly task to remember.

Make sure that the mutual fund you choose is not only low-cost, but also *no-load*. That means that the fund won't charge you anything for buying or selling it. The brokerage might, but the fund won't.

Making investments manually may be a better option if you don't receive a regular salary. You'll gain the ability to use ETFs, which bring tax advantages. The disadvantage to manual investing is that you have to remember to do it.

Use funds based on standard indexes, like the S&P 500, S&P 500 Equal Weight, and Russell 3000. Funds based on more specific indexes are less useful. The *S&P 500 Growth Index*, for example. It's choosier than the S&P 500. It contains stock in large-cap companies, but only those whose revenue and stock price are expected to soar.[1] There are plenty of funds based on it.

Another example is the *S&P 600 Small-Cap Growth Index*. It's pickier still. It also shoots for stock in growth companies, but only small ones.[2] There are funds based on that index, too.

Some might sincerely believe that it's large cap growth stocks that will do best. Others think it's small cap growth stocks that will outperform. In such cases funds based on choosier indexes may seem tempting. But they bring two problems.

First is cost. The more particular the index, the higher the charges. As of this writing the expense ratio of a leading financial institution's S&P 500 Growth ETF is about triple that of its S&P 500 ETF. And its S&P 600 Small-Cap ETF is even pricier. It's five times as much as the standard.[3]

To be sure, both funds are still low cost. As of this writing the expense ratio is 0.10 percent for the large cap growth fund, and 0.15 percent for the small cap growth fund. That's nothing compared to the 1 percent commonly charged by active funds. But higher costs—however mild—still stunt returns.

Second, selective index funds flirt with active management. Of course the funds are still passive. Their managers aren't stock picking. They're just taking orders from the index.

But over at the index company, *someone* is making decisions. Is this a growth company? Is this a small cap? The guidelines for answering such questions can be squishy.

For example, today companies with market capitalizations of under $2 billion would generally be considered small caps. But as of this writing, the biggest stock in the S&P 600 Small-Cap Growth Index has a market cap of over $6 billion.[4] That's three times too big. And yet some crackerjack opted not to boot it.

Of course market caps bop around all the time. Real-time adjustments could be impractical. And index inclusion guidelines may have to be somewhat flexible. So no one can blame the index companies for occasional deviations.

But the more discretion they exercise, the more their choices start to imitate active management. And since passive beats active, that discretion can lead to fund performance that lags. Such are the odds.

Don't sell for the purpose of increasing investment returns. It doesn't work. You have no clue when the market has topped out, and neither do I. Only in retrospect do peaks look predictable. That's why *market timing* is the sport of dingbats. So instead, hold.

Hold also because you're subsidized for doing so. We know that there's generally no tax owed on unrealized capital gains.

Many people choose to invest with sustainability in mind. They want their wealth run ethically. So understandably, they see promise in *impact investing*. It's also known as *SRI*, for *socially responsible investing*; or *ESG*, for *environmental, social, and governance*.

Indexes exist for passive funds that serve that market. The *FTSE U.S. All Cap Choice Index*, for example. It screens out companies that make products like alcohol, tobacco, and weapons. It also excludes outfits that engage in conduct that some consider controversial.[5]

Incidentally, *FTSE* stands for *Financial Times Stock Exchange Group*. It's like a British S&P.

I admire impact investing. People attracted to it have excellent intentions. But they encounter three issues.

First again is cost. Sustainable indexes are selective indexes, so funds based on them charge more. To illustrate, as of this writing a leading ETF based on the FTSE U.S. All Cap Choice index has a 0.12 percent expense ratio. That's quadruple the expense ratio of the same institution's S&P 500 index fund.

Second is definition. People may want to avoid holdings in companies that do bad things. Others may go as far as to only want holdings in companies that do good things. But what exactly is good? What's bad?

Definitions vary. For example, many people see virtue in defending America. They see merit in a strong military. To them, a company that equips the armed forces is admirable. So they might see screening out a domestic weapons manufacturer as ridiculous.

Others might have a very different view of what it means to be responsible. They may champion diversity, for example. They might want holdings in companies led by management teams of varying races and genders, regardless of what products those companies make.

Neither of those definitions is absurd. And that's the problem. Ethics are personal, making impact indexes tricky to construct.

A third problem is imperfection. People make mistakes. And those people work for companies. So the odds that a company tagged as ethical employs only saints is zero.

To illustrate, consider again the FTSE U.S. All Cap Choice Index. Some of the firms in there seem to be tangled up in some scrapes.[6] One, an online media company, is under attack for knowingly harming its users.[7] Another, a technology company, is accused of creating a divisive work environment.[8] Another, a bank, paid its CEO over $30,000,000 last year.[9]

Of course not all impact investors have as their issue user safety, or labor relations, or executive compensation. But many prefer to have portfolios that are free of lapses in these areas.

None of this is to suggest that impact investing shouldn't be pursued. It should be pursued. It's commendable, and on balance probably nudges corporations towards better behavior. But portfolio purity turns out to be an ideal that can only be approached, not secured.

Broad stock market indexes grow nicely. But only over the long term. In the short term, anything could happen. The after-tax return from the S&P 500 may be 7 percent on average. But it's unlikely to be that in any single year.

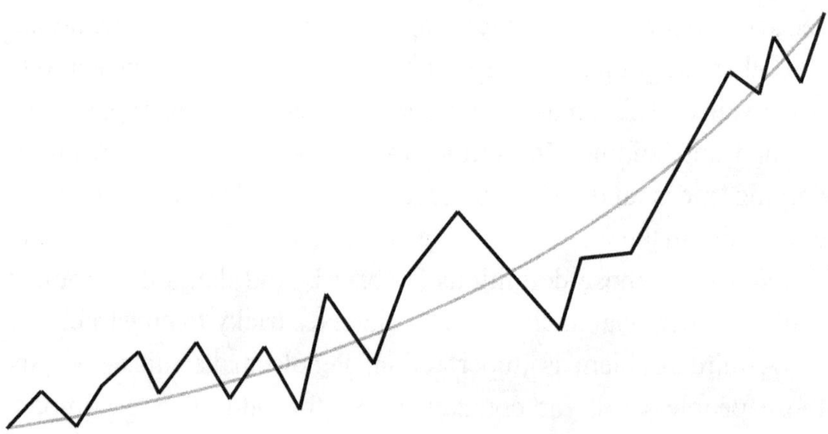

The smooth, light curve is one that we're familiar with. It's the long-term average. But the jagged, dark line better resembles what actually occurs. It shows how volatile stock prices are year-over-year.

Note that during certain intervals one could be fooled into thinking that stocks stink:

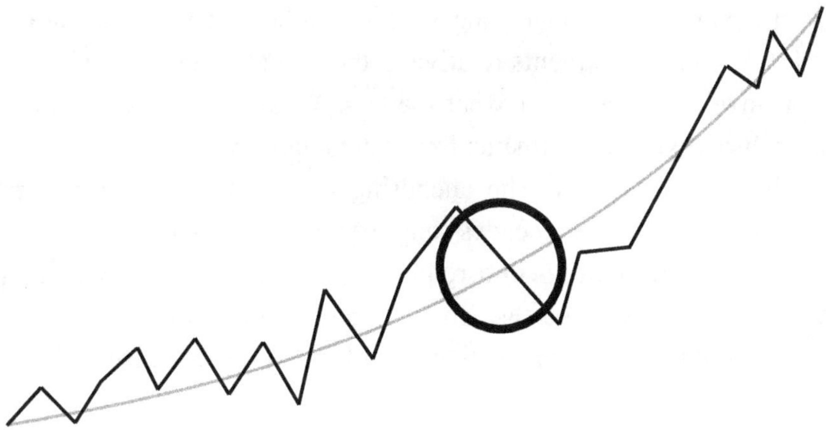

At other times stocks seem fantastic:

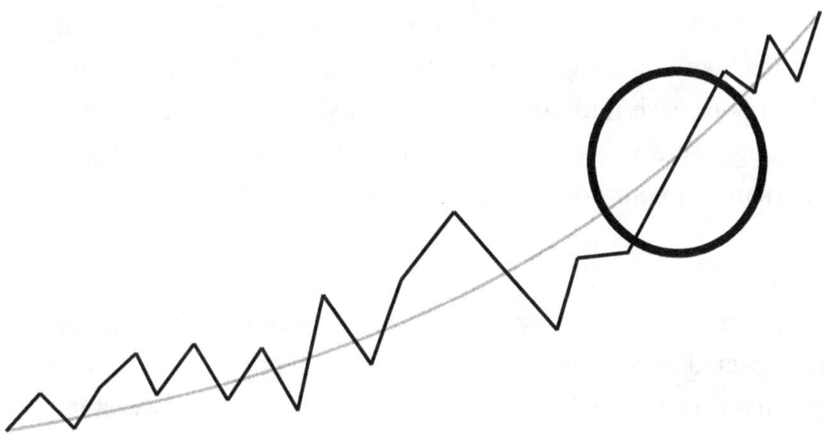

During plunges, it can be tempting to sell the fund. During spikes, it can be tempting to raid your cash buffer and move money from high-yield online savings accounts into the fund. Both impulses are understandable.

But both are misguided. That's because they're driven by the anchoring bias.

In plunges, the anchoring bias spotlights the reduced market price of your investments relative to the higher level from which it just dove. But that's not what matters. What matters is the long-term rise of your investments from years-ago lower levels.

Same with spikes. The anchoring bias highlights recent run-ups. But again, it's decades-long performance that matters. To invest more by cutting into required savings would be wrong. It would chip away at the cash cushion that minimizes your risk.

So ignore short-term stock market blips. They're noise.

Avoid straying from what the odds recommend. You'll receive opportunities to put capital into startups, hedge funds, and real estate. Some people excel with such investments. But most don't.

In the same vein, don't invest in your employer's stock. By all means take advantage of any stock option or RSU programs. But don't pour cash into your firm's listed shares with the intention of holding. We've seen how that increases dependence by handcuffing your portfolio to your job.

At some point you may experience a windfall. You may get an unexpected bonus, inheritance, or other bumper crop of cash. If you have a solid cash buffer and no threatening debt, invest it.

If the windfall is small, it may make sense to invest it all at once. Just be done with it. If it's big, it's okay to dollar cost average your way in. Simply make periodic buys of identical dollar amounts. But only over a short period of time, like a few months. That's because it's pointless to dawdle in low-returning cash while the greener pasture of stocks are sitting right there waiting for you.

As retirement approaches, it may make sense to change how you invest. Specifically it may make sense to put less into stocks, and more into bonds.

We know that bonds tend to return less than stocks. But the income they deliver is steadier, and their market price is more predictable. That consistency can have merit.

How much you should allocate to bonds in retirement largely depends on when in life you mastered personal finance.

If you mastered it early, you may not need many bonds. That's because without them you may still have plenty of cash coming in after you stop working. Those inflows may cover your needs several times over. They'll come from some combination of five sources.

First is payments from taxable brokerage accounts. Those are cash dividends and distributions periodically paid out by ETFs and mutual funds. To someone who started investing decades ago, those payments can be large.

Second is interest from high-yield online savings accounts. That's money thrown off by your cash buffer.

Third is *required minimum distributions*. They're also called *RMD*s. We met them back in chapter 10. They're amounts that older people must withdraw each year from tax-deferred accounts like 401(k)s, 403(b)s, 457(b)s, and non-Roth IRAs.

Since 2020 you're required to take your first RMD by the April 1 following your 72nd birthday. After that, you must take an RMD by December 31 each year. The exact amount varies each time. That's because an RMD is based on an account's balance and your age, both of which change. But it's easy to calculate:

http://www.smallstepstorich.com/21.1.htm

If you're required to take an RMD, take it. That's because the tax for not doing so equals 50% of the RMD.[10]

Fourth is Social Security. It's simple to estimate how much you'll get each month from that outfit:

http://www.smallstepstorich.com/21.2.htm

Fifth is pensions. They're also called *defined benefit plans*. They're increasingly rare. But if you have one, the financial services company that administers it can tell you how much money to expect each month.

Most of these inflows—from taxable brokerage accounts, bank accounts, RMDs, Social Security, and pensions—will be taxed. Some will be taxed at high ordinary income rates. Others, like *qualified dividends* from taxable brokerage accounts, will be taxed at lower long-term capital gains rates. Still others won't be taxed at all. Those include at least 15 percent of Social Security benefits.[11]

If it looks like these after-tax inflows will cover your expenses many times over, bonds might not help much. They'd just make you forego the higher returns of stocks for extra steadiness that you don't need. That could be like using an umbrella during a rainstorm when you're already indoors.

But if you mastered personal finance late, bonds may be more useful. Required minimum distributions may be modest, owing to smaller account balances. Payments from taxable brokerage accounts may be less for the same reason.

Bond investing brings two choices. The first is whether to buy a fund or individual bonds.

Good bond funds have many of the same characteristics of good stock funds. They have low expense ratios, don't charge loads, come from discount brokerages, and are based on broad benchmarks.

It's easy to spot bond funds based on broad benchmarks. They have names that often include the word *total*[12] or *Agg*. Agg is short for *aggregate*. It refers to the Bloomberg Barclays U.S. Aggregate

Bond Index. That's a benchmark for investment grade fixed income securities.[13] It's like an S&P 500 for bonds, with a notable difference.

An S&P 500 fund holds all of the stocks in the S&P 500. But an Agg fund holds only some of the bonds in the Agg. That's necessary, and it's okay. It's necessary because the Agg includes many thousands of different fixed income securities. Some of them don't even trade. So it would be hard for a fund to mirror the Agg. It's okay because it doesn't cause a meaningful gap between the performance of the fund and the Agg.

Suitable bond funds hold only investment grade securities, like those in the Agg. They skip anything that's *junk*, *speculative*, or *high-yield.*

In the context of bank accounts, *high-yield* is a virtue. It means higher return without higher risk, since the FDIC insures the accounts. But with bond funds, high-yield means scary. That's because the FDIC doesn't back them, and the higher potential return comes from the very real risk of default.

Bond fund investing makes good use of two statistics we met back in chapter 14. Both take a stab at the amount of income you might expect from a fund.

The first is the *distribution yield.* Recall that it equals distributions per share over the last 12 months, divided by ending net asset value.

The second is the *30-day SEC yield.* It's the net income received by the fund over the last full month, annualized; divided by the highest price of the fund's shares on the last day of that month.

Both are useful. But they're different. The distribution yield is entirely backward-looking. It measures what happened last year.

The 30-day SEC yield is more forward-looking. It looks at only the last month, and assumes that it will repeat over the next 11. It annualizes the most recent 30 days, basically.

The distribution yield is practical in that it doesn't mess around with conjecture. It just states what happened. But if the economy has changed a lot over the last year, the 30-day SEC yield may be more illuminating. That's because the last month may say more about what's to come than does the last full year.

An additional statistic that pops up in bond fund investing is *duration*. It tries to forecast volatility.

Duration is an estimate of how much the price of a bond fund will change if interest rates change. It's measured in years. A 1 percent change in interest rates is estimated to move the price of the fund 1 percent in the opposite direction for each year of duration.

To illustrate, consider BND. That's the ticker symbol of the Vanguard Total Bond Market ETF. As of this writing it costs $84.80 per share, and has a duration of 6.6.[14] That means that if interest rates suddenly rose 1%, BND would drop to $79.20. That's just $84.80 minus 6.6% of $84.80.

Life is never that clean, of course. For example, interest rates rarely move a full percentage point all at once. Bitty increments are more likely. Further, many things impact bond prices. There's tons of factors, from unemployment rates to crop harvests. So a pure look at the impact of interest rates on bond prices isn't something that reality offers.

But this ain't science. Duration is just an estimate. Its utility comes not from precision. It comes from ballparking how much a bond fund's price may move relative to the variable that impacts it most: interest rates.

The alternative to a bond fund is individual bonds. Buying them brings some of the same complications as buying individual stocks. But fewer. That's largely because bond prices are less volatile. That means fewer opportunities to mess up. Nonetheless, bond picking is still an involved process. It may make the most sense for high income individuals. More on that in a moment.

The second big choice in bond investing is whether to use *taxable* or *tax-exempt* bonds.

Most bonds pay interest that's taxable. But not all. *Munis*, for example. They're issued by state and local governments. We met them back in chapter 14. Their interest is normally tax-free at the federal level. And if you live in the state of the issuer, they're generally tax-free at the state and local level as well.[15]

Income tax exemptions are more useful the higher your tax bracket. We saw this back in chapter 17, with IRA contributions. There's simply more to be saved. So munis tend to work best for those with high incomes during retirement. Discount brokerages offer online tools to help you see if tax-exempt munis make sense for you. For example:

http://www.smallstepstorich.com/21.3.htm

The federal tax exemption is yours regardless of where you live. But the state and local exemptions go only to those living in the state the munis come from. If you're in a populous place like Ohio or California, that's fine. There are low-cost municipal bond funds containing securities issued from only those states.[16]

VNYUX, for example. That's the ticker symbol for the Vanguard New York Long-Term Tax-Exempt Fund.[17] It provides state and local—as well as federal—exemptions to folks all across New York, from Buffalo to the Hamptons.

But for many states there are no low-cost muni funds. Their residents can still have the federal exemption, of course. They can buy shares in a fund focused on only that. VWIUX, for example. That's the Vanguard Intermediate-Term Tax-Exempt Fund. It owns munis from Colorado, Kentucky, Michigan—all over.[18] The federal exemption it can fully deliver. But the state and local it can't. That's when bond picking may make sense: when there's no good alternative. If state and local exemptions are worth a lot to you, and you live in a state without a fund that can do the job, it's reasonable to consider individual munis.

A financial advisor may be helpful here. The advisor would probably construct a muni *bond ladder*. That's a portfolio of bonds that mature at regular intervals. With each maturity comes an opportunity to reinvest at yields that reflect then-prevailing rates. That's good, because it minimizes *interest rate risk*. That's the chance that the price of a bond will fall because of an unexpected rise in interest rates.

Of course financial advisors cost. So before hiring one to pick munis for you, make sure that the cash savings you'll get from the state and local tax exemptions exceed the advisor's fee. If it doesn't, see if your discount brokerage offers an online bond ladder construction tool. Or, consider settling for just the federal exemption with a fund like VWIUX.

If during retirement after-tax cash inflows aren't enough to pay for needs, some combination of four tools may be useful. None is perfect, but all are worth weighing.

One is to take distributions from a Roth IRA. Those aren't taxed.

Second is to withdraw more than the required minimums from tax-deferred accounts. You'll owe more tax, and your account balances will decrease faster. But RMDs are just floors. There's no penalty for taking out more.[19]

Third is to periodically sell some shares in low-cost stock index funds held in taxable brokerage accounts. That's likely to trigger capital gains taxes. But it can raise needed cash.

Fourth is to sell some of those shares not to pay for needs, but rather to buy shares in a low-cost investment grade bond fund. That can replace the variable returns of stocks with the more dependable—albeit smaller—returns of bonds.

If you sell shares in a stock fund, don't use dollar cost averaging. That's because the math that helps when buying hurts when selling. It's easy to see why. Selling to get the same amount of cash each time guarantees that you'll part with more shares on days when the share price is *low*. That's bad. So instead, simply sell when necessary.

Many people set the percentage of their portfolio that's in bonds according to an old rule of thumb. The rule says that it should equal your age. Someone aged 70 would therefore be 70 percent in bonds and 30 percent in stocks.

My opinion is that the rule has merit, but only for setting a maximum. That's for two reasons. First, investment grade fixed income securities currently don't return much. They reflect today's low interest rates.

Second, the rule ignores net worth. Consider two 70 year old retirees. Assume that they have the same Social Security benefits, RMDs, and living expenses. The only difference is the balance in their taxable brokerage accounts. The first has $1,000,000. The second has $10,000,000. The rule suggests that their respective bond allocations should be $700,000 and $7,000,000.

Could that possibly make sense? Does the multimillionaire really need to accept lower returns to secure superfluous steadiness?

No. That's why I think bond allocations should be driven at least as much by net worth as by age.

Three common resources offer to improve your investing. I happen not to use any of them, do-it-yourselfer that I am. But they may make sense for some people under some circumstances.

The first is *target-date funds*. We touched on them earlier. They're also called *life-cycle* funds. They're diversified between asset classes. Each has a different allocation for stock funds and fixed income securities funds.

You're meant to pick a target-date fund that matches your expected year of retirement. If you'll retire in 2050, for example, your fund name ends with something like *target retirement 2050*.

The allocations of a specific target-date fund change over time. As the years pass, the percentage allocated to higher return, higher volatility stocks decreases; and the percentage allocated to lower return, lower volatility bonds increases.

In principle, target-date funds are fine. But they may allocate too much to bonds. Plus their fees can really cut into long-term net performance. That's partly because the funds they use may also charge fees. If you consider them, weigh options from at least three different discount brokerages. Make sure that the funds they use are based on standard indexes, and are low-cost themselves. And verify that any cash balances are FDIC-insured.

A second resource is financial advisors. We've talked about how they can increase dependence, and charge fees that reduce net returns. But some people understandably derive comfort from having a professional look after their economic affairs.

If that's you, consider advisors from at least three different firms. Make sure that they're all fee-only fiduciaries. Such advisors have incentives that are more in sync with yours compared to fee-based non-fiduciaries. Start by searching the directory of registered investment advisors:

http://www.smallstepstorich.com/21.4.htm

Check also the directory of certified financial planners:

http://www.smallstepstorich.com/21.5.htm

While not all RIAs and CFPs are fee-only—you have to ask about that—they are fiduciaries.

Third is *robo-advisors*. They're financial advisory firms that work primarily online, without much human interaction. They combine some features of target-date funds with some features of traditional advisors. There's nothing wrong with them conceptually. But they cost. And as with any investment service, their fees can erase the net benefits they purport to deliver.

Many robo-advisors trumpet their finesse with stunts like *tax-loss harvesting*. That's selling an asset at a loss for the purpose of creating an income tax deduction.

To someone that invests in individual stocks, tax-loss harvesting can be useful. But only somewhat. That's because just a portion of *capital losses* can be used to offset ordinary income. The annual limit is $3,000. The rest can only offset realized capital gains.[20] But one has to sell in order to have realized capital gains. If you hold, you don't.

An infatuation with tax-loss harvesting could even nudge one into speculating. Just knowing that losses have some utility could embolden you into making less sound investments. That's like identifying the best hospital near your house and then getting into an accident for the purpose of becoming a patient.

Tax-loss harvesting—like active management, market timing, and selective indexes—turns out to be more of a distraction than an essential.

Robo-advisors belong to a field of finance called *fintech*. Fintech applies new technology to financial processes. It's promising. But it has yielded two developments that I find puzzling.

The first is cryptocurrencies. We touched on them in chapter 14. They're digital alternatives to cash that aren't issued by governments.

The technology behind cryptocurrencies is clever. Government treasuries may eventually adopt it to issue money without chopping down trees or stamping metal. If they do, that technology could become a standard part of saving. But in 2022 it's hard to see cryptocurrencies as essential to investing.

Much of the interest in cryptocurrencies springs from a distrust of *fiat money*, or government-issued currencies not backed by real assets. The U.S. dollar, for example. It used to be backed by gold. But now it isn't. I appreciate how that could breed concern.

But it's a leap from hating fiat money to loving stateless digital tokens. To me it seems like buying the Swiss franc as if there were no Switzerland, and no franc. I wish the best for those dabbling in this area. But personally, I don't get it.

The second puzzling fintech development is gamified stock brokerages. Their smartphone apps feel like video games, complete with emojis and digital confetti. Some offer the ability to buy fractions of a share instead of whole shares.

Some say that these playful platforms have merit because they introduce young people to investing. I respectfully disagree. What they introduce young people to is speculating. That's as similar to investing as combat is to checkers.

Gamified brokerages make it too easy to slip into the frequent trading and margin buying that create losses. And as for the ability to buy fractional shares, do we need that? After all, most shares already cost well under $100. It's like the tax-loss harvesting gizmo of robo-advisors. It's a feature, but not a benefit. Who cares?

There's a special moment in an investing life. It's when average monthly returns exceed monthly living expenses. You don't detect it instantly. After all, it's after-tax income and not investment returns that covers your costs. But one day you notice that all of the dividends, appreciation, and interest delivered by your portfolio is more than you spend. It's a moment worth envisioning. And the odds are that it's coming.

SUMMARY

1. Start investing once you have the proper level of cash savings and no threatening debt.
2. Invest in low-cost stock index funds.
3. Suitable stock index funds are based on standard indexes like the S&P 500.
4. Any mutual funds used should be no-load.
5. Make investments regularly, either automatically or manually.
6. Invest first through advantaged accounts.
7. Ignore short-term stock price movements.
8. Bonds may be most useful for those with modest income in retirement.
9. Suitable financial advisors are both fee-only and fiduciaries.
10. Any advantages offered by target-date funds and robo-advisors may be eclipsed by fees.
11. When selecting a fund, discount brokerage, or financial professional, always consider at least three different options.

CHAPTER 22

INSURE

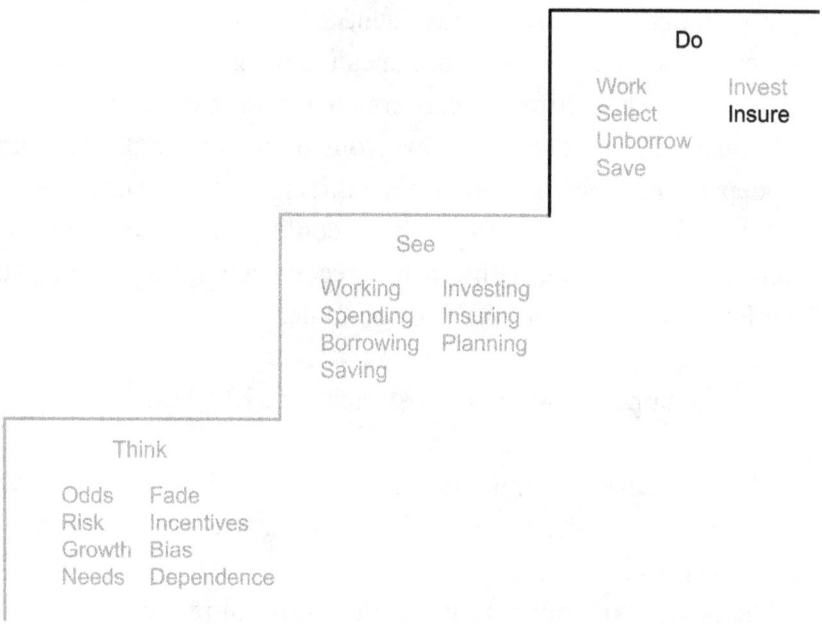

Buy insurance policies that are good. They lower risk.

We've seen how easy it is to spot good insurance policies. They offload big potential expenses that have a reasonable chance of happening, come from financially sound insurers, and charge relatively modest premiums.

Try to buy insurance first through organizations with which you're associated. See if good deals are available through work, a family member's work, or an alumni association. If you're a member of AARP, AAA, or a similar group, check with them. If you have a home outside of the U.S. or are a citizen of another country, see if any insurance you have there covers you in America, or if it can be inexpensively extended to do so.

Even if an organization makes you a great offer, shop around. Get three bids. Try a *captive agent*, who represents just one one insurance company; as well as an *independent agent*, who represents several. Also consider *direct insurance*, offered online by carriers that don't use outside agents.

Getting three bids does not mean having one agent solicit quotes from three different carriers. It means getting bids from three totally different sources. One from an organization, one from an independent agent, and one from a direct insurer, for example.

After identifying a good policy, confirm that the carrier is sound. Check its rating online with a recognized agency like A.M. Best, Fitch, Moody's, or S&P. For example:

http://www.smallstepstorich.com/22.1.htm

Check a carrier's reputation, too. Ask friends if they've ever filed a claim with the insurer. If they have, make sure that they were treated well.

The process of soliciting three bids is useful in part because it refines your requirements. It educates you as to exactly what coverages you need. Plus, it makes you happier after you pick a policy. That's because you never have to wonder whether or not you got the best deal. You saw enough options to know that you did.

Certain policies are essential. Health, for example. Even if you're young and hale, you must have health insurance. In many countries this is automatically provided by the government. But in the U.S. it isn't.

Healthcare costs are so high in America that unexpected medical bills are a leading cause of personal bankruptcy. So don't go an hour without being certain that you're covered. If you don't work for an employer that provides you with health insurance, start your search online:

http://www.smallstepstorich.com/22.2.htm

If you're healthy, have a high income, and have plenty of cash, consider a High Deductible Health Plan (HDHP). Your high tax bracket makes your tax-deductible contributions to a Health Savings Account (HSA) worth a lot. Your large cash buffer means that when you do need medical care you'll easily be able to pay your share. And the returns you earn inside of an HSA will grow tax-free.

But if you have health issues, less income, and a smaller cash buffer, an HDHP isn't for you. You'd likely benefit more from a standard policy.

If an HDHP does make sense and its primary appeal is the HSA, manage the HSA as if it were an IRA. Put it into a low-cost stock index fund. The returns will be yours penalty-free once you turn 65. But the more you need an HSA to pay for qualified medical expenses, the more the HSA should be in cash. Yes, the returns will be less. But otherwise paying for healthcare could be tough should your body and Wall Street conk out at the same time.

Dental insurance is generally separate from health insurance. Consider it. But weigh it against the reasonable alternative of paying for dental care out of pocket.

Once you turn 65, you're eligible for *Medicare*. It's run by the federal government.

Medicare is not free. Parts of it are, and other parts of it are inexpensive. But it costs enough to make understanding it worthwhile. Not riveting, but worthwhile.

Medicare has four parts: A, B, C, and D.

The first is *Medicare part A*. It's also called *hospital insurance*. It's the most basic part, covering hospital stays.

Medicare part A doesn't charge premiums for most Americans and U.S. permanent residents. Specifically, it's free for folks aged 65 or older who have lived in America for at least five years, and who have had Medicare taxes withheld from their paychecks—or their spouse's paychecks—for at least 40 quarters. So it's yours after a decade of employment, basically.

Medicare part A still has copays, and a deductible. In 2021 that deductible was $1,484 per hospital admission. But there aren't any premiums.

Medicare part B is different. It covers doctor visits. It's also called *medical insurance*.

Part B does charge a monthly premium. In 2021 it was $148.50 if your 2019 income didn't exceed either $88,000 or, if you filed a joint tax return, $176,000. The premium is higher if your income was higher:

http://www.smallstepstorich.com/22.3.htm

Part B also has a deductible, and coinsurance. In 2021 the deductible was an annual $203. The coinsurance was 20 percent of charges above the deductible.

Part A plus part B make up what's called *Original Medicare*.

Original Medicare is *public insurance*. It's provided by the government. But the other parts of Medicare aren't. They're *private insurance*. They're regulated by the government, but provided by insurance companies.

Medicare part C, for example. It's also called *Medicare Advantage*. It has all the benefits of parts A and B, and then some. The extras vary by plan. But they can include coverage for things like vision, hearing, and prescription drugs.

Medicare part D is prescription drug coverage by itself. It's available to people that opt for Original Medicare, as opposed to part C.

Same with *Medigap*. It's private insurance that covers deductibles and copays from Original Medicare. It too is available to those who choose Original Medicare instead of plan C.[1]

So starting with Medicare begins with a binary choice: Medicare Advantage, or Original Medicare plus part D and Medigap. The choice depends entirely on your personal situation. The government offers an online tool that may help:

http://www.smallstepstorich.com/22.4.htm

Once your 65th birthday is three months or less away, you're eligible to sign up for Medicare. I am *counting the days*:

http://www.smallstepstorich.com/22.5.htm

If you own a car, auto insurance is mandatory. It's generally required by state law. But even if it wasn't, it would still be needed because car accidents are so common. At a minimum, have liability coverage.

If you have a home mortgage, *homeowners insurance* will also be obligatory. The lender will insist on it. Weigh policies that pay for losses based on *replacement cost* instead of *actual cash value*.

Also consider *flood insurance*. It's generally separate from homeowners insurance. In some cases a mortgage lender may mandate it. In other cases it may be unavailable because of the location of the property. It's easy to check:

http://www.smallstepstorich.com/22.6.htm

If you rent your home, *renters' insurance* may be required by your landlord. If it's not, still consider it. The more guests you have, the wealthier you are, and the more personal property you have in the home, the more useful it is.

If you rely on earned income to support dependents, life insurance is also a must. Under most circumstances *level term* life insurance makes the most sense. Start with quotes on the standard term of 30 years.

Skip *universal life* and *whole life* insurance. We've seen how they both have an investment component that's likely to underperform. If an agent persists in pushing either of those, some commission program has moved the agent's incentives away from yours. Politely excuse yourself and find a different agent.

Of course one needn't die to be unable to work. For this reason *disability insurance* is also worth considering. It replaces part of your earned income if you get sidelined. It's less useful for those who don't rely on earned income to pay for needs. Before buying any policy, see how much disability insurance your state automatically provides.

Lastly, look into *umbrella insurance*. We've seen how it provides liability coverage beyond the limits of other policies. The wealthier you are, the more helpful it is.

As you get three bids for the policies that you need, optimize the quotes. Explore different deductible levels, and eliminate unnecessary coverages.

Consider consolidating policies. If you use one auto insurance company and a family member uses another, get quotes on a single policy that covers you both. If your homeowners insurance and auto insurance come from different carriers, get quotes on a combined policy.

When it comes time to file a claim, first ask yourself if it's worth it. Just because you have coverage doesn't mean you have to use it. Consider paying for small losses out of pocket to avoid the hassle of dealing with the insurance company, and to keep your premiums from increasing.

Be suspicious of insurance that's offered along with some other purchase. Extended warranties, for example. They may cost just a fraction of the price of the refrigerator, speaker system, or dishwasher that you're buying. But as we saw in chapter 15, they often have negative expected values.

Trip cancellation insurance also often falls into this category. There's nothing wrong with it in theory. But for people who tend to complete their itineraries, they're often too expensive to make sense.

Same with insurance offered by car rental companies. They're often too pricey. Plus it's impossible to pore through the nuances of coverage while standing at an airport counter.

Instead consider buying a *non-owner car insurance* policy. It covers your use of cars that you don't own. Check with AAA.

In chapter 15 we saw how auto insurance policies have two components: *liability* and *collision and comprehensive*. Non-owner car insurance policies tackle the liability half. Consider paying for rentals with a credit card that automatically provides the collision and comprehensive half. American Express offers this:

http://www.smallstepstorich.com/22.7.htm

Insurance is unpleasant to consider. It's mundane and exacting, and hands you the treat of picturing yourself maimed, sued, and dead. But it's important. It covers the downside, so that you don't have to visit the downside.

For you, upside.

SUMMARY

1. Buy insurance policies that are good.
2. For any policy, get bids from at least three totally different sources.
3. Never go a moment without health insurance, or any insurance that's required by law.
4. Enroll in Medicare once your 65th birthday is within three months.
5. Before filing an insurance claim, make sure it's worth doing.
6. Be suspicious of insurance that's offered as part of a larger purchase.

CHAPTER 23

GIVE

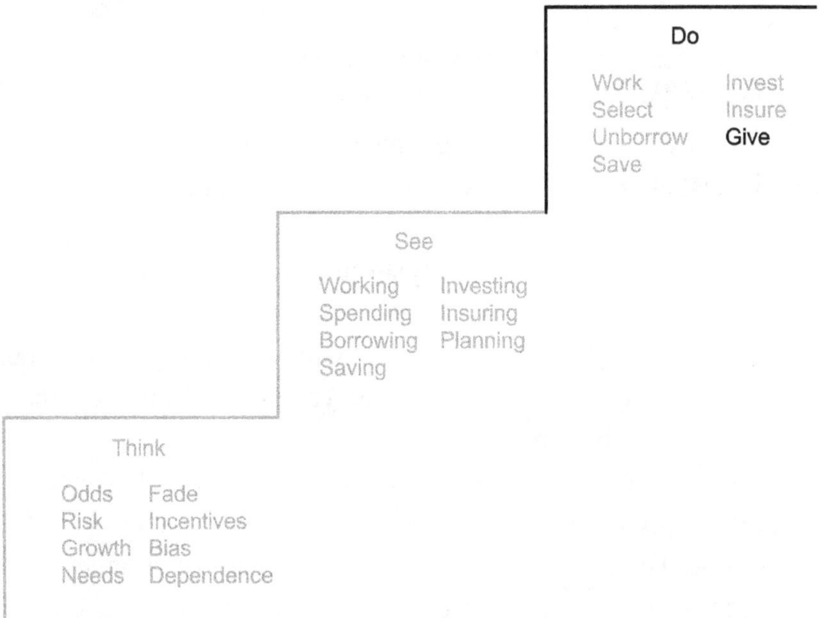

As you master personal finance—as you *work*, *select*, *unborrow*, *save*, *invest*, and *insure*—you amass two things to give to those who will survive you.

The first thing is wealth. Give some of it later, and give some of it now.

Give wealth later by having your assets pass directly to your heirs when you die. Spare your loved ones the trauma of probate. With financial assets like cash and funds, do this with ITF (in trust for) or POD (payable on death) accounts. If an account you had hoped to open can't be made ITF or POD, don't open it. Instead, find one that can at a better financial institution. Make sure that you can name multiple beneficiaries. Then, be sure to name them.

With physical assets like a home, set up a trust. If your estate is likely to stay under the basic exclusion amount—$11,700,000 in 2021 but slated to roughly halve in 2026[1]—use a revocable trust.

If your estate will certainly exceed the basic exclusion amount, look into an irrevocable trust. But because those have consequences that are limiting and permanent, remember that most families find revocable trusts to be more practical.

Your trust could be set up by an attorney—interview three candidates, obviously—or you could do it yourself:

http://www.smallstepstorich.com/23.1.htm

If you own property in a state with a big inheritance tax, consider selling the property before you pass. That may make sense if each of four conditions holds.

First, the property has no sentimental value. It's not the beloved family farm, for example.

Second, you live in a different state, one without an inheritance tax. That would give you the chance to transform real estate that's subject to inheritance tax into cash that isn't.

Third, the property hasn't appreciated. Fair market value isn't above your adjusted basis. That means that a sale wouldn't trigger capital gains tax for you. That's good. And it means that you wouldn't be denying your heirs any stepped-up basis. That's because there'd be no up to step.

Fourth, you can sell the property easily. Perhaps you've already received an offer, or maybe similar properties nearby have recently sold. If you want a real estate agent to help you, interview three candidates before picking one.

ITF accounts and trusts don't solve everything. That's because it's hard to track all of your possessions and routinely update the assets catalogued in the trust. So you may still need a *will*. That document says how you want the rest of your estate distributed. Again it could be written by an attorney, or by you:

http://www.smallstepstorich.com/23.2.htm

Giving some wealth now can also make sense. It can make sense in part because tax law encourages you to do so. In chapter 16 we saw how you can give up to the gift tax exclusion amount to any number of donees annually without owing federal taxes. Since 2018 that amount has been $15,000.[2]

It can also make sense because it reduces the size of your estate. That's helpful if your net worth might otherwise surpass the basic exclusion amount.

If you want to make a gift to someone under age 18, it may be smart to have your discount broker set up an account for them. A *UTMA*, probably. That's a custodial account, owned by a minor but initially run by you. You could put the lucky minor in—surprise!—a low-cost stock index fund.

UTMA stands for *Uniform Transfers to Minors Act*. It's an improvement over the earlier *UGMA—Uniform Gifts to Minors Act*—accounts. That's because UGMAs were more limited in the kinds of assets that they could hold.

Your discount broker shouldn't charge you anything to set up a UTMA account. If they do, question their discountness.

If you give more than the gift tax exclusion amount to anyone in a single year you still might not owe gift tax. You might just reduce your lifetime basic exclusion amount, as we've seen. But you would have to file IRS Form 709. It's straightforward. Unfortunately tax preparation software programs seem not to handle it. So you or your tax preparer get to savor Form 709's lavish prose firsthand:

http://www.smallstepstorich.com/23.3.htm

Recall that if the basic exclusion amount does in fact halve in 2026, you won't be retroactively penalized for having exceeded any new cap that's lower.[3] You won't be fined for having gifted generously.

Nonetheless, don't gift too much. Don't put yourself in a position where you might become strapped for cash. If you have the instinct to do so, I salute your benevolence. But it would be silly to have to go to your heirs for money later just because you had the good fortune to live longer than expected.

Before you make gifts in the form of contributions to a 529 plan, make sure that the beneficiary is likely to have future tuition expenses. That's hard to gauge years in advance, obviously. But sometimes there's a big fact worth weighing.

Consider for example children with dual citizenship. They're Americans. But they're also citizens of a country where university may be free or inexpensive. If they study abroad they might never owe any tuition, even if they go on to get a PhD.

If a 529 does make sense, set one up. Make contributions to it, and invest those contributions. If school costs are more than a decade away, put the balance in a low-cost stock index fund. As tuition bills draw near, transition to cash. My opinion is that the cash balance in a 529 account should equal the next four years worth of qualified education expenses. That way the student won't struggle to pay tuition if stocks decide to cycle down.

Bonds may be useful here as well. If school expenses are less than 10 years away but more than four years away, perhaps some of the 529 should be in a low-cost investment-grade bond fund. That's likely to return more than cash, as we know. But it shouldn't bop around in price as much as a stock fund. Once education costs are less than four years away, start selling the bond fund for cash.

That cash can be withdrawn tax-free to pay for qualified education expenses. Those include tuition, fees, required textbooks, computers used for school, and standard room and board. But some costs are excluded. They're *nonqualified.* They include transportation, sports, associations, health insurance, and student loan costs.

Sometimes the balance in a 529 doesn't get spent. Returns in the account may have been sufficiently high that an amount remains after graduation. Or perhaps the beneficiary winds up not going to school at all.

In either case the goal becomes to use the balance without incurring taxes or penalties. One way to do this is by changing the beneficiary. Just name another member of the original beneficiary's family to someone who's likely to have future school costs.

As a last resort, a lingering 529 balance can be withdrawn for nonqualified purposes. Boat repairs, pedicures—anything. The returns will be subject to income tax, plus a 10% penalty. But at least the original contributions will escape unscathed.[4]

There are times when the last thing one wants to focus on is money. When a spouse dies, for example. That's a trying period, one when there are much more important matters to think about. But after some weeks it makes sense to attend to practicalities.

IRS Form 706, for example. It can be used to transfer to you any DSUE. That's the *deceased spousal unused exclusion* that we saw earlier.[5] It's smart to use even if your estate is well under the basic exclusion amount, which was $11,700,000 in 2021. That's for two reasons.

First, some asset you own could spike in price before your death. An S&P 500 index fund, for example. Remember 2019? That year the S&P 500 raced up over 30 percent.[6] An estate owned by someone who died that December could have made use of all the exclusion it could get.

Second, the basic exclusion amount is slated to drop. It may, or it may not. But if it does, DSUEs will plunge. So one might as well accept the generosity of Form 706 while it's in a good mood.

Tax preparation software programs seem not to handle Form 706. So have it filled out by your tax preparer, or brave it yourself:

http://www.smallstepstorich.com/23.4.htm

The second thing you can give to those who will survive you is more important than wealth. It's good judgment.

You know how to practice personal finance well. Show that way to your heirs. Don't preach; that doesn't work. *Show*. Lead by example. Let them see how you spend consciously, invest regularly, and work happily. That increases the odds that they'll adopt your good ways on their own accord.

When they do, they'll benefit. But so will you. That's because they may come to manage your affairs.

As we age, we lose some mental sharpness. We do what we can to delay that inevitability for as long as possible. But at some point the cognitive lights start to flicker. That's when it may make sense to hand the money reins over to someone else. That someone is now yours to mentor.

It's best if that someone truly loves you. Otherwise, money-grabbers disguised as helpers can pop out of the woodwork. I've witnessed two such situations.

In one, a groundskeeper got his entire family hired in various do-nothing jobs by an older person, and then tried to get the older person to name them all as beneficiaries of the estate. Fortunately an astute relative of the older person was paying attention. The relative got a court to bar the groundskeeper's family from ever contacting the older person again.

In another, a retiree hired an estate lawyer—a longtime acquaintance—to prepare a will for a reasonable fee. But after the retiree died the lawyer persuaded a court to increase that fee sixfold. It was all legal, but unambiguously crafty. The lawyer turned out to be a practiced expert at this deception, having done it many times.

Some people are desperate. They may be indebted, addicted, or just plain misoriented. They're motivated to prey on soft targets. And they may feel justified in doing so. For example, the groundskeeper—an addict—felt the original beneficiaries unworthy. Same with the estate lawyer. He lived in the same religious community as the retiree, a community that was wary of non-members.

It's a shame how such undercurrents can make despicable conduct seem fine in the eyes of the perpetrator. But they can.

Those were unfortunate episodes. But they highlight how useful it can be to bring a younger loved one along on your personal finance journey. It increases the odds that you'll pass the reins to able hands.

During their lifetimes your heirs may see economic conditions that you never did. They may see a wealth tax, negative interest rates, or a stock index scandal. It's hard to predict if any of these things will happen, and if they do, how they might play out.

But please know that I've written this book with such eventualities in mind. I've tried to encourage a mental orientation that's robust, one that should work in different financial environments. The numbers are certain to adjust. Annual gift tax exclusions, conforming mortgage loan limits, and IRA contribution maximums will all change. But the right mindset won't. It's durable. It's the same mindset that guides my choices, choices that I put on display for my own children.

Estate planning is personal. Understandably, people make different decisions. Take gifts. Some people give the maximum tax-free amount to their heirs every year. Others give nothing with the sincere intent of encouraging initiative. Still others give the maximum to heirs that demonstrate competence with money, and less to heirs that don't.

It's not for me to tell you which approach is right. What is for me to tell you is this: *give more good judgment than wealth*. Because if you do, eventually there'll be more of both.

SUMMARY

1. Give both wealth and good judgment to your heirs.
2. Give wealth later with ITF accounts, a trust, and a will.
3. If you give wealth now, take advantage of the annual gift tax exclusion.
4. Give good judgment by exhibiting your sound personal finance practices.
5. Give more good judgment than wealth.

THE SMALL STEPS TO RICH

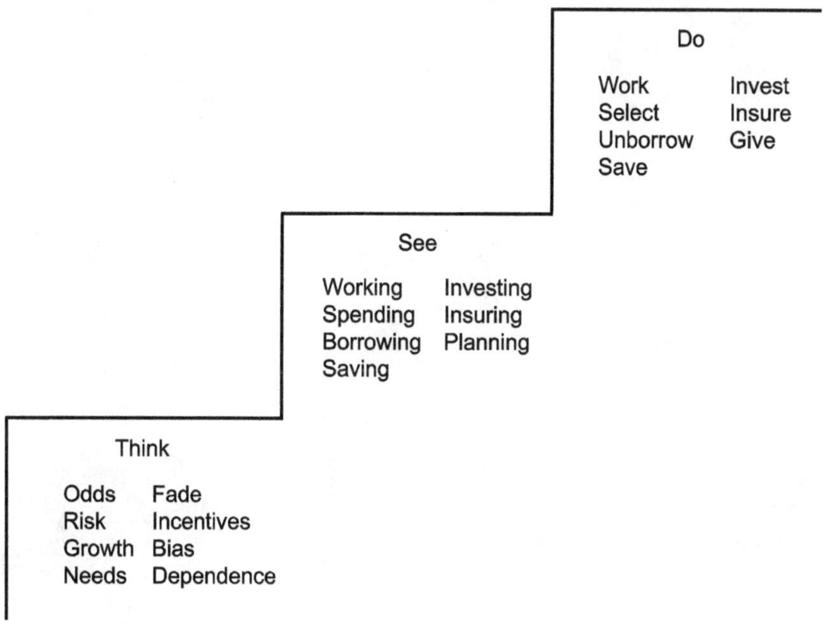

GLOSSARY

7-day effective yield

Annualized yield based on *income* from the last seven days, with the effect of *compounding*; as with a *money market fund.* Also called *effective yield.*

7-day yield

Annualized yield based on *income* from the last seven days, without the effect of *compounding*; as with a *money market fund.*

30-day SEC yield

A *fund* performance ratio. The numerator equals *dividends* and *interest* received by the fund, minus the fund's operating expenses; based on the most recent full month, *annualized.* The denominator is the highest price of the fund's *shares* on the last day of that month.

401(a)

An employer-sponsored advantaged account designed for employees of government, education, and non-profit organizations, who generally require participation.

401(k)

An employer-sponsored advantaged account that often features *matching contributions*, designed for employees of private sector companies.

403(b)

An employer-sponsored advantaged account that may feature *matching contributions*, designed for employees of public schools and non-profit organizations.

457(b)

An employer-sponsored advantaged account that usually does not feature *matching contributions*, designed for government employees.

529

A *tax-advantaged* account designed to pay for school.

706

An *IRS* form used for *estate tax* purposes, such as to transfer a *DSUE* to a surviving spouse.

709

An *IRS* form used for *gift tax* purposes, such as to report gifts exceeding the annual *gift tax exclusion.*

1099

An *IRS* form that reports the earnings of an *independent contractor*. Distinct from a *W-2*, which reports the earnings of an *employee*.

5329

An *IRS* form used to report penalties related to *qualified* plans like *IRAs*.

8606

An *IRS* form used to report non-*deductible contributions* to a *traditional IRA* and conversions from a traditional to *Roth IRA*.

8938

An *IRS* form used to report non-U.S. financial assets. Also called a *Statement of Specified Foreign Financial Assets*.

AAR

The rate of *return* that, had it been achieved each year, would have delivered the same end result that the more *volatile* annual returns actually did. Commonly used to compare *funds*. Short for *average annual return.*

APR

Yearly *interest* divided by *balance* excluding *compounding*, as with a *debt*. Short for *annual percentage rate*.

APY

The yearly *yield* of an *asset* including intra-year *compounding*, as with a *bank* account. Short for *annual percentage yield.*

ARM

A *loan secured* by *real estate* whose *interest rate* is *fixed* for an initial period and *floating* thereafter. Short for *adjustable-rate mortgage*. An alternative to a *fixed-rate mortgage*.

AUM

The total market value of *assets* managed, in a *fund* or otherwise. Short for *assets under management*.

Accredited investor

An individual that has pre-*tax income* over $200,000 for each of the last two years, a *net worth* excluding primary residence over $1,000,000, or any of several professional designations. Distinct from *qualified purchaser*.

Active

The characteristic of a *fund* that means it's not based on an *index*. The alternative to *passive*.

Actual cash value

An *insurance policy* settlement *term* calling for a *carrier* to pay *depreciated* value instead of the higher *replacement cost*.

Adjustable-rate mortgage

A *loan secured* by *real estate* whose *interest rate* is *fixed* for an initial period and *floating* thereafter. Shortened to *ARM*. An alternative to a *fixed-rate mortgage*.

Adjusted basis

The total original purchase price of an *asset* plus items like improvements and minus items like *depreciation*. Also called *adjusted cost basis* or *tax basis*.

Adjusted cost basis

The total original purchase price of an *asset* plus items like improvements and minus items like *depreciation*. Also called *adjusted basis* or *tax basis*.

Adjusted expense ratio

The annual operating expenses of a *fund*, less fee waivers, reimbursements, *interest* expenses, and *dividend* expenses; expressed as a percentage of the fund's *assets*. Equal to or less than the *net expense ratio* and the *gross expense ratio*.

Adverse selection

A scenario where one party is attracted to a transaction for a reason that should repel the other party.

Affinity bias

The mental tendency to want things one likes for inessential reasons.

Agent

A party hired by a *principal* to achieve some end.

Agg

Short for the Bloomberg Barclays U.S. Aggregate Bond Index, a *benchmark* for *investment grade fixed income securities.*

Amortization

The process of reducing the *principal* on a *loan* by making periodic payments.

Amortization schedule

A table showing how much of each periodic payment on a *loan* reduces *principal*, and how much is *interest* expense.

Anchoring bias

The mental tendency to *benchmark* against insignificant baselines.

Angel investing

Buying *stock* in *startups*, generally by individuals; and often before the startups have received *venture capital*.

Annual percentage rate

Yearly *interest* divided by *balance* excluding *compounding*, as with a *debt*. Shortened to *APR*.

Annual percentage yield.

The yearly *yield* of an *asset* including intra-year *compounding*, as with a *bank* account. Shortened to *APY*.

Annualized

Stated in yearly terms but based on data from a shorter period, as with a quarterly *dividend* multiplied by four.

Annuity

An *investment* product offered by *insurance* companies that promises to make a stream of future payments.

Appraiser

A professional estimator of the *fair market value* of *real assets* like *real estate*.

Appreciation

Increase in price or value over time, generally of a tangible *asset* like a house. The opposite of *depreciation*.

Arithmetic mean

The sum of a set of numbers divided by the number of numbers in the set.

Asset

Something owned and of value. Often used as a synonym for *investment*, *holding*, or *security*.

Asset allocation

The process of apportioning wealth among different *asset classes*.

Asset class

A group of *assets* with similar characteristics, such as *stocks*, *fixed income securities*, *cash*, and *real assets*.

Assets under management

The total market value of *assets* managed, in a *fund* or otherwise. Shortened to *AUM*.

Authority bias

The mental tendency to follow leaders unthinkingly.

Automatic investing

A program of buying *securities* at regular intervals with a set amount of *cash* each time.

Availability bias

The mental tendency to make decisions based on information that's easily recalled as opposed to most relevant.

Average annual return

The rate of *return* that, had it been achieved each year, would have delivered the same end result that the more *volatile* annual returns actually did. Commonly used to compare *funds*. Shortened to *AAR*.

Backdoor Roth IRA

The process of making non-*deductible contributions* to a *traditional IRA* that is then converted into a *Roth IRA*.

Back-end load

An extra fee paid by an investor when selling an *asset*, such as certain *mutual funds*.

Balance

An amount of *money*. With *bank* and *brokerage* accounts, the amount in an account. With *debt*, the amount still owed.

Balloon

The characteristic of a *loan* indicating that it does not fully *amortize* by *maturity*, requiring the borrower to make a large final payment. Also used to describe that payment.

Bank

A regulated, for-profit financial institution that accepts deposits and makes *loans*.

Basic exclusion amount

The amount of an *estate* not subject to *estate tax*, equal to $11,700,000 in 2021.

Basis

Short for *adjusted basis*, *adjusted cost basis*, *cost basis, stepped-up basis*, and *tax basis*.

Basis point

One one hundredth of 1 percent. Also called *BPS*. Commonly pronounced in the plural, as "bips."

Behavioral economics

The study of how psychology impacts *economic* decision making.

Benchmark

A quantitative standard, often based on an *index*, to which actual *returns* are compared.

Beneficiary

A designated recipient, for example of a *life insurance policy death benefit*.

Bequest

An amount of wealth distributed in accordance with a *will*.

Bias

A flawed mental shortcut.

Blue-chip

Large and established, as with a *corporation* or its *stock*.

Bond

A financial *asset* that promises to pay set amounts like *interest* and *principal*. Also called a *fixed income security*.

Bond ladder

A *portfolio* of *fixed income securities* that *mature* on different dates, creating periodic *liquidity*.

Borrowing

A financial *liability* that generally incurs *interest* and must be paid back. Also called *debt* or *leverage*.

Broker

A person or company that intermediates the sale and purchase of *assets*, particularly *securities* or *real estate*.

Broker-dealer

A company that intermediates the sale and purchase of *securities*, and that buys and sells securities for its own account.

Brokerage

A company that intermediates the sale and purchase of *assets*, particularly *securities* or *real estate*. Also called *broker*.

Budget

A plan to spend within set limits.

Bubble

A period of time when certain *asset* prices climb to unjustifiable heights, ending with an abrupt fall.

Buying rate

The amount of one currency that a buyer is willing to pay for a different currency. A version of an *exchange rate*, the alternatives being the *mid-market rate* and the *selling rate*.

CAGR

An annual growth rate that captures the effect of *compounding*. Short for *compound annual growth rate*.

CD

A *bank* deposit that pays a *fixed interest rate*, and that cannot be withdrawn without penalty before a set date. Also called *certificate of deposit*, *time deposit* or *term deposit*.

CDIC

The Canadian government agency that guarantees Canadian *bank* deposits, as the *FDIC* does in the U.S. Short for *Canada Deposit Insurance Corporation*.

COBRA

A *health insurance* program that lets individuals buy continued *coverage* after leaving employment. Short for *Consolidated Omnibus Budget Reconciliation Act*.

CPA

Someone licensed to provide accounting services by a state board of accountancy. Short for *certified public accountant*.

Canada Deposit Insurance Corporation

The Canadian government agency that guarantees *bank* deposits, as the *FDIC* does in the U.S. Shortened to *CDIC*.

Capital

Money or other *assets*.

Capital gain

The amount realized from the sale of an *asset* minus *adjusted basis*, when positive. The opposite of *capital loss*.

Capital loss

The amount realized from the sale of an *asset* minus *adjusted basis*, when negative. The opposite of *capital gain*.

Capitalization-weighted

The characteristic of a *stock index* indicating that the proportion allocated to each holding varies with *market capitalization*. Also called *market-weighted*. An alternative to *equal-weighted*.

Captive agent

An *insurance agent* that represents a single insurance company, unlike an *independent agent*.

Carrier

An *insurance* company. Also called *underwriter*.

Cash

Legal tender issued by governments. Also called *money*.

Cash equivalents

Securities readily convertible into *cash* at full value, such as *Treasurys*.

Cash management account

An alternative to a *bank checking account* or *money market account*, offered by *brokerages*. Also called *CMA*.

Cash value

The accumulated worth of an *insurance policy* that has an *investment* component, such as *universal life insurance* or *whole life insurance*.

Cash-out refinance

A *refinancing* that replaces an existing *mortgage* and provides the borrower with *cash*.

Cashpoint

The British word for ATM, or automated teller machine.

Catch-up contribution

The increased amount that people age 50 or older can put in advantaged accounts like *401(k)s* and *IRAs*.

Certificate of deposit

A *bank* deposit that pays a *fixed interest rate*, and that cannot be withdrawn without penalty before a set date. Also called *CD*, *time deposit* or *term deposit*.

Certified public accountant

Someone licensed to provide accounting services by a state board of accountancy. Shortened to *CPA*.

Checking account

The traditional *bank* alternative to a *brokerage cash management account* or *money market account*, used for everyday purposes like receiving salaries and paying bills.

Claim

A formal request by a *policyholder* to an *insurance* company for payment to cover an event such as an accident or illness.

Closed-end fund

A *fund* that raises *money* through an *IPO* with a *fixed* number of *shares* that subsequently trade on a *stock exchange*. The alternative to an *open-end fund*.

Closet indexing

Actively managing a *fund* in a way that's indistinct from *passive* management, often resulting in a higher *management fee* than would be charged by a functionally similar *index* fund.

Closing

The last step in a transaction, generally when a buyer makes the final payment to a seller in exchange for *title*.

Closing costs

The sum of expenses paid at the inception of a *loan*, particularly a *mortgage*.

Coinsurance

The percentage of the cost of a medical service owed by a *health insurance policyholder* above the *deductible*.

Collateral

An *asset* pledged to *secure* a *loan* that can be seized by the lender in the event of *default*.

Collision and comprehensive

The portion of an auto *insurance policy* that *covers* damage to the *policyholder's* vehicle. Distinct from *liability*.

Commercial paper

Unsecured debt issued by established *corporations* that has an original time to *maturity* of less than 9 months. Part of the *money market*.

Commodity

A basic good from agriculture, mining, or energy that is an input in production processes. A type of *real asset*.

Compound annual growth rate

An annual growth rate that captures the effect of *compounding*. Also called *CAGR*.

Compound yield

Annualized yield with the effect of *compounding*, as with a *money market fund*. Also called the *effective yield*.

Compounding

The effect of one period's *return* increasing the amount on which the next period's return is based.

Concentration

The allocation of wealth among few *assets* or *asset classes*. Also called *focus*. The opposite of *diversification*.

Confirmation bias

The mental tendency to favor ideas that support one's preexisting views.

Conforming

The characteristic of a *mortgage* indicating that it meets *Federal Housing Finance Agency* guidelines, usually resulting in a lower *interest rate*.

Consensus bias

The mental tendency to want things just because they're popular.

Consistency bias

The mental tendency to favor actions that are in concert with prior actions.

Consolidated Omnibus Budget Reconciliation Act

The law that created *COBRA*, the *health insurance* program that lets individuals maintain *coverage* after leaving employment.

Contractor

Someone who works for an organization who is not an *employee*, who receives a *1099* instead of a *W-2*. Also called an *independent contractor*.

Contribution

An amount put into an advantaged account like an *IRA*.

Copayment

A *fixed* amount paid by a *health insurance policyholder* for a medical service.

Corporation

A common type of business entity, where ownership is represented by *shares* of *stock*. Can be either *public* or *privately held*.

Correlated

Quantitatively related, as with the price of two different *stock index funds*.

Cost basis

The total original purchase price of an *asset*.

Coupon

Interest paid on a *fixed income security*, expressed either in currency or as an annual percentage of *par value*.

Coupon rate

Interest paid on a *fixed income security*, expressed as an annual percentage of *par value*. Also called *nominal yield*. Distinct from *current yield*.

Coverage

The extent of the *insurance* provided by a *policy*. Also called *protection*.

Coverdell ESA

A *tax-advantaged* account designed to pay for education, more oriented towards elementary and secondary school than a *529*.

Creation unit

A block of *shares* in an *ETF*.

Credit

Allowed *debt* capacity. Separately, an addition to an account.

Credit report

A summary of an individual's *debt* and bill payment history.

Credit score

A number between 300 and 850 that represents an individual's *creditworthiness*. Also called *FICO* score.

Credit union

A regulated, not-for-profit financial institution that accepts deposits and makes *loans*.

Creditworthy

Safe to lend to; likely to pay back borrowed amounts based on a high *credit score* and a good *credit report*.

Cryptocurrency

A digital alternative to *cash* that is not issued by a government.

Current yield

Annualized payments received from an *asset* divided by the current price of that asset, as with a *fixed income security*.

Custodial account

An account at a financial institution owned by a *minor* and managed by an adult.

Custodian

The manager of a *custodial account*. Separately, a financial institution that holds *assets* on a client's behalf.

DICGC

The government agency in India that guarantees *bank* deposits, as the *FDIC* does in the U.S. Short for *Deposit Insurance and Credit Guarantee Corporation*.

DJIA

An *equal-weighted index* of *stock* in 30 *large capitalization* U.S. companies. Short for *Dow Jones Industrial Average*.

DSUE

The portion of a deceased spouse's *basic exclusion amount* that may be transferred to the surviving spouse. Short for *deceased spousal unused exclusion*.

DTI

A factor lenders use to determine *creditworthiness*. Calculated as monthly *debt* payments divided by monthly *gross income*. Short for *debt-to-income ratio*.

Daily balance method

Calculating *interest* by multiplying the daily *balance* by the *annual percentage rate* and then dividing by the number of days in a year.

Death benefit

The payout to a *beneficiary* of a *life insurance policy* upon the death of an insured person.

Debt

A financial *liability* that generally incurs *interest* and must be paid back. Also called *borrowing* or *leverage*. Relatedly, a synonym for *fixed income security*.

Debt-to-income ratio

Monthly *debt* payments divided by monthly *gross income*. A factor lenders use to determine a potential borrower's *creditworthiness*. Also called *DTI*.

Deceased spousal unused exclusion

The portion of a deceased spouse's *basic exclusion amount* that may be transferred to the surviving spouse. Shortened to *DSUE*.

Deductible

In *insurance*, an amount paid *out-of-pocket* before a *carrier* starts paying. In *tax*, the characteristic of an amount that means it reduces *taxable income*. Short for *tax-deductible* in that context.

Default

Failure to fulfill an obligation, particularly to pay *interest* or *principal* on a *debt*.

Defined benefit plan

An employer-funded plan designed to finance retirement. Also called a *pension*. Distinct from a *defined contribution plan*.

Defined contribution plan

An employee-funded program designed to finance retirement, like a *401(k)* or a *403(b)*. Distinct from a *defined benefit plan*.

Deflation

A decline in the general level of prices. Less common than its opposite, *inflation*.

Deposit Insurance and Credit Guarantee Corporation

The government agency in India that guarantees *bank* deposits, as the *FDIC* does in the U.S. Shortened to *DICGC*.

Depreciation

Decrease in price or value over time, generally of a tangible *asset* like a car. The opposite of *appreciation*.

Diminishing marginal returns

The concept from *economics* that each additional unit of an *asset returns* less than did the last.

Diminishing marginal utility

The concept from *economics* that each additional unit of something is less useful than was the last.

Direct insurance

Policies offered by *carriers* that don't sell through outside *agents*.

Direct rollover

The *tax*-free transfer of *assets* from one advantaged account into another, as with a *401(k)* into an *IRA*.

Disability insurance

A contract that calls for a *carrier* to pay part of the lost *income* of a *policyholder* that is unable to work, generally in exchange for *premiums*.

Discount points

Fees paid to a *mortgage* lender at *closing* to lower the *interest rate*, generally by 25 *basis points* per discount point. One discount point generally costs 1 percent of the mortgage amount. Often shortened to *points*.

Disregarded entity

An entity that shares a *tax* identity with a taxpayer, as a *revocable trust* does with a *grantor*.

Distribution

A periodic payment from a *fund*. Separately, a withdrawal from an advantaged account like a *401(k)*.

Distribution yield

A *fund* performance ratio. The numerator equals *distributions* per *share* over the last 12 months. The denominator equals *NAV* at the end of those 12 months. Also called *trailing 12-month yield* or *TTM yield*.

Diversification

The practice of allocating wealth among different *assets* or *asset classes*. The opposite of *concentration*.

Dividend

A payment made by a *corporation* or *fund* to its shareholders, generally in *cash* and on a periodic basis.

Dividend yield

The *annualized dividend* from a *share* divided by the share's current price.

Dollar cost averaging

Investing the same amount of *money* in a *listed security* at set time intervals for the purpose of lowering average cost.

Donee

The recipient of a *gift*.

Donor

The giver of a *gift*.

Dow Jones Industrial Average

An *equal-weighted index* of *stock* in 30 *large capitalization* U.S. companies. Shortened to *DJIA*.

Down payment

An initial *cash* payment made towards a purchase, often expressed as a percentage of the full price.

Draw

Borrow from a *line of credit*. More generally, to take *money* out of an account.

Dry powder

Cash waiting to be *invested* in *assets* like *stocks*.

Duration

An estimate of the effect that a change in *interest rates* will have on the price of a *fixed income security* or fixed income security *fund*. Measured in years. A 1 percent change in interest rates is estimated to move the price by negative 1 percent times duration.

ESG

An approach to *investing* that prioritizes ethics. Short for *environmental, social, and governance*. Similar to *SRI*, or *socially responsible investing*; and *impact investing*.

ETF

A *fund* that invests in *securities* and that trades throughout the day on a *stock exchange*. Short for *exchange-traded fund*. An alternative to a *mutual fund*.

Earned income

Money made by working, generally *taxed* at the *ordinary income* rate.

Economics

A social science concerned with the production and consumption of goods and services.

Education savings plan

A *529* plan where wealth earmarked for school expenses can earn untaxed *returns*. The alternative to the less common *prepaid tuition plan*.

Effective tax rate

Tax liability divided by *taxable income*. An average that results from different tax rates applying to different tiers of a taxpayer's income.

Effective yield

Annualized yield with the effect of *compounding*, as with a *money market fund*. Also called the *compound yield*.

Election

A *tax* choice made deliberately as opposed to by default, such as the transfer of a *DSUE* to a surviving spouse.

Employee

Someone who works for an organization who is not an *independent contractor*, who receives a *W-2* instead of a *1099*.

Equal-weighted

The characteristic of a *stock index* indicating that the proportion allocated to each holding is the same. An alternative to *market-weighted*.

Equifax

One of the three big U.S. *credit* reporting agencies, along with *Experian* and *Transunion*.

Equity

An ownership stake in a *corporation*. Also called *stock* or *shares*. Separately, market price minus *loan balance*, as with *real estate*.

Escrow

The stage of a transaction where *cash* from a buyer is held by a third party for disbursement to a seller when certain conditions are met, as with *real estate*.

Estate

The total *net assets* of a person, generally used in the context of *estate planning.*

Estate planning

The process of optimizing one's financial affairs in anticipation of eventual death.

Estate tax

A *tax* on the transfer of *assets* of a deceased person, generally paid for by that person's *estate*. Distinct from *inheritance tax*.

Excess contribution

The amount over the allowed limit put into an advantaged account like an *HSA* or *IRA*.

Exchange control

A law restricting the purchase, sale, or movement of a country's currency.

Exchange rate

The price of a currency expressed in a different currency.

Exchange-traded fund

A *fund* that invests in *securities* and that trades throughout the day on a *stock exchange*. Shortened to *ETF*. An alternative to a *mutual fund.*

Exercise

To buy a *stock* or other *security* with an *option.*

Exercise price

The stipulated cost to buy a *stock* or other *security* through an *option*. Also called the *strike price*.

Expected value

The probability of something happening multiplied by the payoff if it does in fact happen.

Expense ratio

A measure of the cost efficiency of a *fund*. Annual operating expenses expressed as a percentage of the fund's *assets*.

Experian

One of the three big U.S. *credit* reporting agencies, along with *Equifax* and *Transunion*.

FBAR

A federal government form that must be filed annually by Americans with certain financial accounts outside of the U.S. Short for *Report of Foreign Bank and Financial Accounts*.

FDIC

The U.S. government agency that guarantees U.S. *bank* deposits. Short for *Federal Deposit Insurance Corporation*.

FHFA

A government agency that oversees parts of the *mortgage* market. Short for *Federal Housing Finance Agency*.

FSA

An advantaged account provided by an employer to pay for a specified category of expense, like healthcare. Also called *flexible spending account* or *flexible spending arrangement*. An alternative to an *HSA*.

FSCS

The British government agency that guarantees *bank* deposits, as the *FDIC* does in the U.S. Short for *Financial Services Compensation Scheme*.

FTSE

A British *index* provider comparable to *S&P* in the U.S. Short for *Financial Times Stock Exchange Group*.

Face value

Money that the *issuer* of a *fixed income security* is meant to repay at *maturity*. Also called *par value* or *principal*.

Fair market value

The price at which a buyer and a seller—both willing, informed, and unrushed—would exchange an *asset*.

Federal funds rate

The *interest rate* that U.S. *banks* charge each other for overnight *loans*.

Federal Housing Finance Agency

A government agency that oversees parts of the *mortgage* market. Shortened to *FHFA*.

Fee-based

The designation of a *financial advisor* that may be paid by promoters of *investment* products as well as advisory clients. An alternative to *fee-only*.

Fee-only

The designation of a *financial advisor* that is paid only by clients, not by promoters of *investment* products. An alternative to *fee-based*.

Fiat money

Government-issued currencies that are not backed by *real assets* like gold.

Fiduciary

A person or entity that is obligated to manage client *assets* in a way that best serves the client.

Finance charge

Any fee or *interest* expense incurred as a result of *borrowing*.

Financial advisor

A professional paid to manage the financial affairs of clients.

Financial Services Compensation Scheme

The British government agency that guarantees *bank* deposits, as the *FDIC* does in the U.S. Shortened to *FSCS*.

Financial statement

A quantitative history of a business, such as an income statement, cash flow statement, or balance sheet.

Financial Times Stock Exchange Group

A British *index* provider comparable to *S&P* in the U.S. Shortened to *FTSE*, and pronounced "footsie."

Fintech

An emerging industry that applies technology to financial processes.

Fixed

Unchanging over time, as with the *interest rate* on a *CD*. The opposite of *floating* or *variable*. Relatedly, a set dollar amount, as with a *copayment*.

Fixed annuity

An investment product offered by *insurance* companies that promises set rates of *return*. An alternative to an *indexed annuity* or *variable annuity*.

Fixed income security

A *bond*, *note*, or other *asset* that evidences a *borrowing*, and that promises to pay back predetermined amounts like *interest*. Commonly referred to as a *debt* or *bond*.

Fixed-rate mortgage

A *loan secured* by *real estate* whose *interest rate* and monthly payments stay the same throughout the *term* of the *mortgage*. An alternative to an *adjustable-rate mortgage*.

Flexible spending arrangement

An advantaged account provided by an employer to pay for a specified category of expense, like healthcare. Also called *flexible spending account* or *FSA*. An alternative to an *HSA*.

Floating

Changeable, like the *interest rate* on an *adjustable-rate mortgage*. Also called *variable*. The opposite of *fixed* or *pegged*.

Focus

The allocation of wealth among few *assets* or *asset classes*. Also called *concentration*. The opposite of *diversification*.

Front-end load

An extra fee paid by an investor when buying an *asset*, such as certain *mutual funds*.

Fund

A *portfolio* of *capital* meant to be invested according to some theme or strategy.

Fundamental analysis

A method of evaluating *stocks* that focuses on individual *corporations* as opposed to general trends or economic conditions.

Gain

Market price minus cost, generally described as either *realized* or *unrealized*.

Gift

A transfer of wealth from *donor* to *donee* without the donor receiving anything of equal value in return.

Gift tax

A *tax* on wealth given away, generally not due on amounts up to the *gift tax exclusion*, and generally paid by the *donor*.

Gift tax exclusion

An amount not subject to *gift tax* that can be given to a *donee* annually, equal to $15,000 since 2018.

Grantor

The creator of a *trust*. Also called *settlor* or *trustor*.

Grantor trust

A *trust* that shares a *tax* identity with its *grantor*, making it a *disregarded entity.* The alternative to a *non-grantor trust*.

Gross

Before subtracting amounts like deductions, expenses, *liabilities*, reimbursements, waivers, or *withholding*. The opposite of *net*.

Gross expense ratio

The total annual operating expenses of a *fund* expressed as a percentage of the fund's *assets*. More than or equal to the *net expense ratio*.

Gross income

Money earned before subtracting any deductions or *tax* expenses. Distinct from *net income*.

Growth investing

An *active* strategy that emphasizes buying *assets* that are likely to increase in value over time.

HDHP

A health *insurance policy* that qualifies one to contribute to an *HSA*. Short for *High Deductible Health Plan*.

HMO

The aspect of a health *insurance* plan that requires *policyholders* to use certain medical service providers. Short for *health maintenance organization*. An alternative to a *PPO*.

HSA

An advantaged account designed to pay for medical costs not covered by a *High Deductible Health Plan*. Short for *Health Savings Account*.

Hard credit inquiry

A check of a *credit report* that negatively impacts *credit score* and that will appear on future credit reports. Also called a *hard pull*. The alternative to a *soft credit inquiry*.

Hard pull

A check of a *credit report* that negatively impacts *credit score* and that will appear on future credit reports. Also called a *hard credit inquiry*. The alternative to a *soft pull*.

Health maintenance organization

The aspect of a health *insurance* plan that requires *policyholders* to use certain medical service providers. Shortened to *HMO*. An alternative to a *preferred provider organization*.

Health Savings Account

An advantaged account designed to pay for medical costs not covered by a *High Deductible Health Plan*. Shortened to *HSA*.

Hedge fund

A *portfolio* of *capital* meant to be invested according to some theme or strategy, generally *private* and managed more ambitiously than an *ETF* or *mutual fund.*

High Deductible Health Plan

A health *insurance policy* that qualifies one to contribute to an *HSA*. Shortened to *HDHP*.

High net worth individual

An affluent person, generally with financial assets exceeding $1,000,000.

High-yield

The characteristic of a *bank* account that means it offers a high *interest rate*. Separately, the characteristic of a *fixed income security* indicating a general expectation that *interest* and *principal* may not be paid as promised. Also called *junk*, *non-investment grade*, or *speculative* in that latter context.

Holding

Something owned and of value. Often used as a synonym for *asset*, *investment*, or *security*.

Holding period

The period of time an *asset* was owned, often used to characterize a *capital gain* as either *short-term* or *long-term*.

Home equity line of credit

A *line of credit secured* by a home. Also called a *HELOC*.

Home insurance

A *policy* that *covers* the structures, personal *property*, and *liabilities* of a private residence owner. Also called *homeowners insurance*.

Homeowners insurance

A *policy* that *covers* the structures, personal *property*, and *liabilities* of a private residence owner. Also called *home insurance*.

IPO

The first sale of a *stock* on a *stock exchange*, with proceeds generally going to the *issuer*. Short for *initial public offering*.

IRA

A category of advantaged accounts designed to finance retirement, including a *Roth IRA*, *SEP IRA*, and *traditional IRA*. Short for *individual retirement account*.

IRS

The U.S. federal *tax* agency. Short for *Internal Revenue Service*.

ITF

The characteristic of an account that lets it pass easily to a *beneficiary* upon the death of its owner. Short for *in trust for*. Also called *payable on death* or *POD*.

Illiquid

Not readily convertible into *cash* without penalty. Opposite of *liquid*.

Impact investing

An approach to *investing* that prioritizes ethics. Similar to *SRI* and *ESG*.

In-the-money

The characteristic of an *option* that means its *exercise price* is less than the price of the *security* it can be used to buy.

In trust for

The characteristic of an account that lets it pass easily to a *beneficiary* upon the death of its owner. Also called *ITF*, *payable on death*, or *POD*.

Incentive fee

A periodic charge to investors in a *fund* based on *returns* instead of *assets under management* or *net asset value*. Also called a *performance fee*. Distinct from a *management fee*.

Income

Money earned from work and *investments*.

Income tax

Money due to a government based on *income*, generally calculated as a percent of that income.

Independent agent

An *insurance agent* that represents multiple *carriers*, unlike a *captive agent*.

Independent contractor

Someone who works for an organization who is not an *employee*, who receives a *1099* instead of a *W-2*. Often shortened to *contractor*.

Index

A *benchmark* or standard, such as the *S&P 500* for *stocks* and the *prime rate* for *debt*.

Index fund

A *fund* that is *passive*.

Indexed annuity

An investment product offered by *insurance* companies that promises a *return* based on both a guaranteed minimum and the performance of an *index* such as the *S&P 500*. An alternative to a *fixed annuity* or a *variable annuity*.

Individual retirement account

A category of advantaged accounts designed to finance retirement, including a *Roth IRA*, *SEP IRA*, and *traditional IRA*. Shortened to *IRA*.

Inflation

An increase in the general level of prices. More common than its opposite, *deflation*.

Inheritance tax

A *tax* paid by heirs on *assets* received from the *estate* of a deceased person. Distinct from *estate tax*.

Initial public offering

The first sale of a *stock* on a *stock exchange*, with proceeds generally going to the *issuer*. Shortened to *IPO*.

Installment

A type of *loan* that requires periodic payments until the *principal* is zero. Also used to describe one such payment. An alternative to *revolving*.

Insurance

A contract that calls for a *carrier* to provide *coverage* to a *policyholder*, generally in exchange for *premiums*.

Interest

An amount periodically paid on a *balance*. Separately, an ownership stake in a *partnership*.

Interest rate

An amount periodically paid on the *balance* of a *bank* account, *debt*, or *fixed income security*; generally expressed as an *annualized* percentage.

Interest rate risk

The chance that the price of a *fixed income security*, or fixed income security *fund*, will fall because of a rise in *interest rates*.

Internal Revenue Service

The U.S. federal *tax* agency. Shortened to *IRS*.

Investing

Committing wealth in pursuit of a *return*.

Investment

An *asset* purchased in pursuit of a *return*. Relatedly, the amount of *money* spent on such a purchase. Often used as a synonym for asset, *holding*, or *security*.

Investment grade

The characteristic of a *fixed income security* indicating that *interest* and *principal* are generally expected to be paid as promised. The opposite of *non-investment grade*.

Irrevocable trust

A legal entity established by a *grantor* to own *assets* like a home for the purpose of passing ownership to a *beneficiary* without *probate*, where the beneficiary controls the contributed assets. An alternative to a *revocable trust*.

Issuer

An entity that creates and sells *securities*, like a city that issues *munis* or a *corporation* that issues *stock*.

Itemized deductions

Expenses listed on a *tax return* that reduce taxable *income*. The alternative to the *standard deduction*.

Jumbo

The characteristic of a *mortgage* indicating that it is *nonconforming* because it is too large.

Junk

The characteristic of a *fixed income security* indicating a general expectation that *interest* and *principal* may not be paid as promised. Also called *high-yield*, *non-investment grade*, or *speculative*.

LIBOR

The *interest rate* that big international *banks* charge each other for short-term *loans*. A common *index* for *debt*. Pronounced "lie bore." Short for *London Interbank Offered Rate*.

LTV

A maximum set by lenders, equal to *debt* over value. In real estate, the *mortgage* amount divided by *appraised* value. Short for *loan-to-value ratio*.

Large capitalization stocks

Shares in companies with big *market capitalizations*, generally over $10 billion. Shortened to *large caps*.

Large caps

Shares in companies with big *market capitalizations*, generally over $10 billion. Short for *large capitalization stocks*.

Lease

A contract where a *lessee* pays a *lessor* to use an *asset* like *real estate*, generally for a predetermined period that's longer than with a *rental* agreement. Relatedly, the act of leasing.

Lessee

The party that pays the *lessor* in a *lease*.

Lessor

The party that owns the *asset* in a *lease*.

Level load

An extra annual fee paid by an investor for owning an *asset*, such as certain *mutual funds*.

Level term

Term life insurance with *premiums* that stay the same over time.

Leverage

A financial *liability* that generally incurs *interest* and must be paid back. Also called *borrowing* or *debt*.

Liability

An obligation or amount owed, such as the *balance* on a *debt*. Separately, a category of *insurance* that covers claims resulting from damage to *property* or people.

Lien

The right that a lender has to *collateral*.

Life-cycle fund

A *fund* that deliberately shifts its *asset allocation* away from *stocks* and towards *fixed income securities* over time. Also called a *target-date fund*.

Life expectancy factor

One of two main determinants of a *required minimum distribution*, the other being account *balance*.

Life insurance

A *policy* that calls for a *carrier* to pay a *death benefit* to a *beneficiary* upon the death of an *insured* person, generally in exchange for *premiums*.

Limit order

An investor's instruction to a *broker* to buy a *security* at or below a specified price, or to sell a security at or above a specified price. An alternative to a *market order*.

Line

A category of *insurance*, such as *property* or *life*.

Line of credit

A standing opportunity to repeatedly borrow and repay *money* up to some limit. Similar to *revolving credit.*

Liquid

Cash, or readily convertible into cash without penalty. Opposite of *illiquid*.

Liquid net worth

Cash plus *cash equivalents* minus *liabilities*. Used as a strict measure of solvency. Generally smaller than *net worth.*

Listed

Traded on an exchange, as with *stock* on a *stock exchange*. Also called *public*.

Living trust

A *trust* established during the lifetime of the *grantor*.

Load

An extra fee charged to investors to buy or sell certain *mutual funds*.

Loan

An amount of *money* given by one party to another with the expectation that it will be returned, generally with *interest*.

Loan-to-value ratio

A maximum set by lenders, equal to *debt* over value. In real estate, the *mortgage* amount divided by *appraised* value. Shortened to *LTV*.

London Interbank Offered Rate

The *interest rate* that big international *banks* charge each other for short-term *loans*. A common *index* for *debt*. Shortened to LIBOR, pronounced "lie bore."

Long-term capital gain

A *capital gain* from the sale of an *asset* owned for more than a year, generally subject to a lower *tax* rate than a *short-term capital gain.*

MAGI

A common measure of personal *income* used for various qualifications, such as the *tax deductibility* of *contributions* to a *traditional IRA*. Short for *modified adjusted gross income*.

MMA

An alternative to a *bank checking account* or *cash management account*, offered by *brokerages*. Short for *money market account*.

Management fee

A periodic charge to investors in a *fund* based on *assets under management* or *net asset value* instead of *returns*. Distinct from a *performance fee*.

Margin

A *loan* made by a *brokerage*, *secured* by the borrower's own *capital* at the brokerage.

Margin account

An account that lets a *brokerage* client borrow on *margin*.

Margin call

A requirement by a *brokerage* that a *margin account* client post more *collateral*, usually because of a drop in the price of *securities* bought on *margin*.

Marginal return

The incremental *return* from an additional unit of an *asset*.

Marginal utility

The incremental benefit delivered by one more unit of something.

Market cap

The theoretical price for all of the *equity* of a *public* company, calculated as *shares outstanding* times the current share price. Short for *market capitalization*.

Market capitalization

The theoretical price for all of the *equity* of a *public* company, calculated as *shares outstanding* times the current share price. Shortened to *market cap*.

Market order

An investor's instruction to a *broker* to buy or sell a *security* at the best available price. An alternative to a *limit order*.

Market timing

An *investing* tactic based on predictions of future price movements.

Market-weighted

The characteristic of a *stock index* indicating that the proportion allocated to each holding varies with *market capitalization.* Also called *capitalization-weighted.* An alternative to *equal-weighted.*

Marketable

The characteristic of a *security* meaning that it can be bought and sold on a *public* exchange.

Matching contribution

Money an employer puts into an advantaged account like a *401(k)* or *403(b)* in some proportion to the employee's own *contribution.*

Maturity

The time when the *principal* of a *fixed income security* or *debt* is meant to be repaid.

Mean reversion

The concept that performance measures tend towards historical averages, as with *returns* from an *asset class*.

Medicaid

The U.S. *public insurance* plan designed to provide healthcare to people with low *incomes*. Distinct from *Medicare*.

Medicare

The U.S. *public insurance* plan designed to provide healthcare to people aged 65 and older. Distinct from *Medicaid.*

Medicare Advantage

Private insurance that offers the benefits of *Medicare part A* and *Medicare part B*, plus additional *coverage* such as vision, hearing, and prescription drugs. Also called *Medicare part C*.

Medicare part A

The basic portion of *Medicare*, covering hospitalizations. Also called *hospital insurance*. Makes up *Original Medicare* along with *Medicare part B*.

Medicare part B

The portion of *Medicare* that covers doctors' appointments. Also called *medical insurance*. Makes up *Original Medicare* along with *Medicare part A*.

Medicare part C

Private insurance that offers the benefits of *Medicare part A* and *Medicare part B*, plus additional *coverage* such as vision, hearing, and prescription drugs. Also called *Medicare Advantage*.

Medicare part D

Private insurance that covers prescription drugs for people enrolled in *Original Medicare*.

Medigap

Private insurance that helps cover the *deductibles* and *copays* of *Original Medicare*.

Mid-market rate

An *exchange rate*, specifically the midpoint between the *buying rate* and the *selling rate*.

Modified adjusted gross income

A measure of personal *income* used for various qualifications, such as the *tax deductibility* of *contributions* to a *traditional IRA*. Shortened to *MAGI*.

Modified duration

Duration expressed as a percentage.

Momentum investing

An *active* strategy that emphasizes buying *securities* that have recently increased in price, based on the view that they'll continue to increase in price.

Money

Legal tender issued by a government. Also called *cash*. Relatedly, an economic amount.

Money market

The segment of the *fixed income securities* market consisting of *marketable*, short-term, low *credit risk securities* like *Treasury bills*, *certificates of deposit*, and *commercial paper*.

Money market account

An alternative to a *bank checking account* or *cash management account*, offered by *brokerages*. Shortened to *MMA*. Also called *money market deposit account* or *money market savings account*.

Mortgage

A *loan secured* by *real estate*.

Mortgage points

Fees paid to a *mortgage* lender at *closing*, either as *origination fees* or as *discount points* to lower the *interest rate*. One point generally costs 1 percent of the mortgage amount. Often shortened to *points*.

Muni

A *fixed income security* issued by a local government, featuring *interest* exempt from some *tax*. Short for *municipal bond*.

Municipal bond

A *fixed income security* issued by a local government, featuring *interest* exempt from some *tax*. Shortened to *muni*.

Mutual fund

A *fund* that invests in *securities* and that trades just once a day on a *stock exchange*. An alternative to an *ETF*.

NAV

The *assets* minus *liabilities* of a *fund*, generally expressed on a per-*share* basis. Short for *net asset value*.

NCUA

The U.S. government agency that guarantees U.S. *credit union* deposits. Short for *National Credit Union Administration*.

National Credit Union Administration

The U.S. government agency that guarantees *credit union* deposits. Shortened to *NCUA*.

Negative amortization

The process of increasing the *principal* on a *loan* by making periodic payments that aren't even big enough to cover *interest* expense.

Negative marginal utility

The incremental harm delivered by one more unit of something.

Neobank

A *bank* that operates primarily online, generally without physical branches.

Net

Minus an amount of something, such as deductions, expenses, *liabilities*, reimbursements, waivers, or *withholding*.

Net asset value

The *assets* minus *liabilities* of a *fund*, generally expressed on a per-*share* basis. Shortened to *NAV*.

Net assets

Assets minus *liabilities*, often used to describe the financial condition of an individual or a family. Also called *net worth*.

Net expense ratio

The annual operating expenses of a *fund*, minus fee waivers and reimbursements; expressed as a percentage of the fund's *assets*. Less than or equal to the *gross expense ratio*.

Net income

Money earned after subtracting any deductions or *tax* expenses. In the context of employment, also called *take-home pay*. Distinct from *gross income*.

Net worth

Assets minus *liabilities*, often used to describe the financial condition of an individual or a family. Also called *net assets*.

No cash-out refinance

A *refinancing* that replaces an existing *mortgage* without providing the borrower with *cash*. Also called a *rate and term refinance*. An alternative to a *cash-out refinance*.

No-load

Without extra fees charged to investors to buy or sell, as with *mutual funds*.

Nominal

Not adjusted for price, *tax*, or *inflation*. In the context of inflation, the opposite of *real*.

Nominal yield

Interest paid on a *fixed income security*, expressed as an annual percentage of *par value*. Also called *coupon rate*. Distinct from *current yield*.

Non-grantor trust

A *trust* that has its own *tax* identity, distinct from its *grantor*. The alternative to a *grantor trust*.

Non-investment grade

The characteristic of a *fixed income security* indicating a general expectation that *interest* and *principal* may not be paid as promised. Also called *high-yield, junk*, or *speculative*. The opposite of *investment grade*.

Non-owner car insurance

Auto *liability insurance* designed for people who drive but don't own a car.

Nonconforming

The characteristic of a *mortgage* indicating that it doesn't meet *Federal Housing Finance Agency* guidelines, usually resulting in a higher *interest rate*.

Nonqualified distribution

A withdrawal from an *IRA* or other advantaged account that is subject to penalty. The opposite of a *qualified distribution*.

Nonqualified dividend

A *dividend* subject to the *ordinary income tax* rate, as distinct from *qualified dividends* that are subject to the lower *long-term capital gains* tax rate. Also called *ordinary dividend.*

Nonqualified mortgage

A *loan secured* by *real estate* that doesn't meet federal government standards of affordability, usually resulting in a higher *interest rate*. While distinct from a *nonconforming mortgage*, a mortgage can be both nonqualified and nonconforming.

Open-end fund

A *fund* that regularly issues and redeems *shares* at *net asset value*, like most *mutual funds*. The alternative to a *closed-end fund*.

Opportunity cost

The concept from *economics* that sees making a choice as creating an expense in the form of the foregone benefits of alternatives.

Option

A *security* that gives the holder the right to buy, or sell, a *stock* or other security at a predetermined price for a specified *term*.

Ordinary dividend

A *dividend* subject to the *ordinary income tax* rate, as distinct from *qualified dividends* that are subject to the lower *long-term capital gains* tax rate. Also called *nonqualified dividend*.

Ordinary income

Income taxed at the relatively high ordinary income tax rate, generally from working, *interest*, *nonqualified dividends*, and *short-term capital gains*.

Original Medicare

Medicare part A plus *Medicare part B*.

Origination fee

A fee paid to a *mortgage* lender at *closing* for arranging the *loan*, often set at some percentage of the mortgage amount. Also called *origination points*.

Origination points

A fee paid to a *mortgage* lender at *closing* for arranging the loan, often set at some percentage of the mortgage amount. Also called *origination fee*.

Out-of-pocket

The characteristic of an expense that means it's paid with one's own *money*, as with the *deductible* of an *insurance policy*.

Out-of-the-money

The characteristic of an *option* that means its *exercise price* is more than the price of the *security* it can be used to buy. Also called *underwater*.

Outlier

A data point that is extreme relative to the other data points in the set.

Outstanding amount

Money owed on a *debt,* or due from a *fixed income security*, that isn't *interest*. Also called *balance* or *principal*.

Over-the-counter

The characteristic of a *security* that means that it is traded, but not on an organized exchange. Also called *OTC*.

Overdraft

A *loan* from a financial institution triggered by a withdrawal in excess of an account *balance*.

PMI

An *insurance policy* that a *mortgage* lender may require of a homebuyer that makes a *down payment* of less than 20 percent. Short for *private mortgage insurance*.

POD

The characteristic of an account that lets it pass easily to a *beneficiary* upon the death of its owner. Short for *payable on death*. Also called *in trust for* or *ITF*.

PPO

The aspect of a health *insurance* plan that charges *policyholders* less for using certain medical service providers. Short for *preferred provider organization*. An alternative to an *HMO*.

Par value

Money that the *issuer* of a *fixed income security* is meant to repay at *maturity*. Also called *face value* or *principal*.

Partnership

A type of business entity where ownership is represented by *interests*. Often *privately held*.

Pass-through deposit insurance

FDIC deposit *insurance* obtained through a non-*bank* financial institution, such as a *brokerage*.

Passive

The characteristic of a *fund* that means it's based on an *index*. The opposite of *active*.

Payable on death

The characteristic of an account that lets it pass easily to a *beneficiary* upon the death of its owner. Also called *POD*, *in trust for*, or *ITF*.

Payback period

The amount of time it takes to recoup an *investment*, without considering the *time value of money*.

Pegged

The characteristic of an *exchange rate* that means unchanging over time. Also called *fixed*. The opposite of *floating* or *variable*.

Pension

An employer-funded plan designed to finance retirement. Also called a *defined benefit plan*.

Performance fee

A periodic charge to investors in a *fund* based on *returns* instead of *assets under management* or *net asset value*. Also called an *incentive fee*. Distinct from a *management fee*.

Points

A fee paid to a *mortgage* lender at *closing*, either as *discount points* to lower the *interest rate*, or as an *origination fee*. One point generally costs 1 percent of the mortgage amount. Also called *mortgage points*, and—confusingly—often used as shorthand for *discount points*.

Policy

A contract between an *insurance* company and a *policyholder*.

Policyholder

An owner of an *insurance policy* or *annuity*.

Portable

An *estate planning* concept meaning transferable from deceased spouse to surviving spouse, as with a *DSUE*.

Portfolio

A collection of *holdings*, often among different *asset classes*.

Preapproval letter

A document from a *mortgage* lender showing a homebuyer's ability to borrow a certain amount.

Preferred provider organization

The aspect of a health *insurance* plan that charges *policyholders* less for using certain medical service providers. Shortened to *PPO*. An alternative to a *health maintenance organization*.

Premium

The price of an *insurance policy* or *annuity*. Separately, an excess amount paid.

Prepaid tuition plan

A *529* plan where tuition is paid in advance. The alternative to the more common *education savings plan*.

Prepayment penalty

A charge for paying off a *mortgage* early.

Present value

A stream of future cash flows discounted back at some rate such that it can be expressed as a single amount in current terms.

Preservation of capital

An investment posture that prioritizes not losing *money* over maximizing *return.*

Prime rate

The *interest rate* that *banks* charge their most *creditworthy borrowers*. A common *index* for *debt*.

Principal

Money owed on a *debt*. Also called *balance* or *outstanding amount*. Relatedly, money that the *issuer* of a *fixed income security* is meant to repay at *maturity*. Also called *face value* or *par value* in that context. Separately, a party that hires an *agent* to achieve some end.

Principal-agent problem

The difference in incentives between one party and another party hired by the first to achieve some end.

Private

Not *listed* on a *stock exchange*, as with a *hedge fund*. Separately, not from a government, as with *private insurance*.

Private insurance

Insurance provided by a *corporation* or other non-government entity. An alternative to *public insurance*.

Private mortgage insurance

An *insurance policy* that a *mortgage* lender may require of a homebuyer that makes a *down payment* of less than 20 percent. Shortened to *PMI.*

Privately held

The characteristic of a company that means that its *stock* is not traded on a *stock exchange*. Also called *private*.

Probate

A complex legal process that results in the distribution of the *assets* of a deceased person's *estate*.

Pro-rata rule

The *IRS* rule stating that the *tax*-free portion of a *distribution* from a *traditional IRA* depends on the percentage of total *contributions* to that IRA that were made with after-tax dollars.

Property

Land and buildings. A kind of *real asset*. Also called *real estate*. Relatedly, a synonym for *asset*.

Property tax

A periodic *tax* on *real estate*, generally based on *appraised* value.

Protection

The extent of the *insurance* provided by a *policy*. Also called *coverage*.

Public

Traded on an exchange, as with *stock* on a *stock exchange*. Also called *listed*. Separately, of or related to government.

Public insurance

Insurance provided by a government, as with *Medicare*. An alternative to *private insurance*.

Purchasing power

The amount of goods and services that a unit of *money* can buy, generally reduced over time by *inflation*.

Qualified

Allowed by rule or granted preferential treatment, as with educational expenses that may be paid for with *529* plan withdrawals.

Qualified distribution

A withdrawal from an *IRA* or other advantaged account that is not subject to penalty. The opposite of *nonqualified distribution*.

Qualified dividend

A *dividend* subject to the *long-term capital gains tax* rate, as distinct from *nonqualified dividends* that are subject to the higher *ordinary income* tax rate.

Qualified mortgage

A *loan secured* by *real estate* that meets federal government standards of affordability, usually resulting in a lower *interest rate*. While distinct from a *conforming mortgage*, a mortgage can be both qualified and conforming.

Qualified purchaser

An individual or family business that owns at least $5,000,000 in investments. Distinct from *accredited investor*.

REIT

A type of *real estate* entity that distributes at least 90 percent of its *taxable income* to *shareholders* in the form of *dividends*. Short for *real estate investment trust*.

RMD

The amount that people must withdraw from *tax-deferred* accounts each year, starting at age 72 since 2020. Short for *required minimum distribution*.

RRSP

A Canadian advantaged account comparable to a *401(k)*. Short for *Registered Retirement Savings Plan*.

RSU

A *security* that gives the holder *stock* in the *issuer* after a *vesting period*. Short for *restricted stock unit*.

Rate and term refinance

A *refinancing* that replaces an existing *mortgage* without providing the borrower with *cash*. Also called *no cash-out refinance*. An alternative to a *cash-out refinance*.

Real

Adjusted for *inflation*. The opposite of *nominal*. Separately, a class of *assets* whose worth comes from their physical properties.

Real assets

Assets whose worth comes from their physical properties, like *commodities* and *real estate*. An *asset class*.

Real estate

Land and buildings. A kind of *real asset*. Also called *property*.

Real estate investment trust

A type of *real estate* entity that distributes at least 90 percent of its *taxable income* to *shareholders* in the form of *dividends*. Shortened to *REIT*.

Realized

Actualized through a sale, as in a *realized gain*.

Rebalancing

The practice of maintaining *target allocations* by periodically buying and selling *assets* like *securities*.

Reciprocity bias

The mental tendency to treat others as they have treated us.

Refinancing

Replacing an old *debt* with a new debt that has better *terms*, such as a lower *interest rate* or lower monthly payments. Shortened to *refi*.

Registered Retirement Savings Plan

A Canadian advantaged account comparable to a *401(k)*. Shortened to *RRSP*.

Rent

To pay to use another's *asset* like *real estate*, generally for a predetermined period that's shorter than with a *lease*. Relatedly, a payment made under a rental agreement.

Renters' insurance

A *policy* that covers the personal *property* and *liabilities* of a residential *real estate* tenant.

Replacement cost

An *insurance policy* settlement *term* calling for a *carrier* to pay to replace property, without any deductions for *depreciation.* An alternative to *actual cash value*.

Report of Foreign Bank and Financial Accounts

A federal government form that must be filed annually by Americans with certain financial accounts outside of the U.S. Shortened to *FBAR*.

Required minimum distribution

The amount that people must withdraw from *tax-deferred* accounts each year, starting at age 72 since 2020. Shortened to *RMD*.

Restricted stock unit

A *security* that gives the holder *stock* in the *issuer* after a *vesting period.* Shortened to *RSU.*

Return

Money made on an *asset*, often stated as an *annualized* percentage of the price of that asset. Separately, a periodic filing with a *tax* authority.

Revocable trust

A legal entity established by a *grantor* to own *assets* like a home for the purpose of passing ownership to a *beneficiary* without *probate,* where the grantor controls the contributed assets while alive. An alternative to an *irrevocable trust*.

Revolving

A type of *credit* that provides an opportunity to repeatedly borrow and repay *money* up to some limit. Similar to *line of credit.* An alternative to *installment*.

Risk

The chance of loss, conventionally quantified by price *volatility*.

Risk-return trade-off

The conventional idea that higher potential *returns* come from accepting greater price *volatility*.

Rollover

The transfer of *assets* from one account into a similar account, as with a maturing *CD* into a new CD.

Roth IRA

An advantaged account designed to finance retirement, withdrawals from which aren't *taxed* within certain parameters.

Round

A stage of financing of a *startup* or other *privately held* company.

Russell 3000

A *capitalization-weighted index* of *stock* in the 3,000 U.S. companies with the largest *market capitalizations*.

S&P

A provider of *indexes* such as the *S&P 500*. Short for *Standard and Poor's*.

S&P 500

A *capitalization-weighted index* of *stock* in approximately 500 *large capitalization* U.S. companies.

SEC

The U.S. federal *securities* markets regulator. Short for *Securities and Exchange Commission.*

SEP IRA

An advantaged account designed to finance retirement, *contributions* to which are *tax-deductible* for the employer that makes them. Short for *simplified employee pension individual retirement account.*

SIPC

A non-profit *corporation* that helps clients retrieve *assets* from *broker-dealers* that fail. Short for *Securities Investor Protection Corporation.*

SIPP

A British advantaged account comparable to a *401(k)*. Short for *self-invested personal pension.*

SRI

An approach to *investing* that prioritizes ethics. Short for *socially responsible investing*. Similar to *ESG* and *impact investing.*

Sampling

A *passive fund* management tactic of including only some components of an *index* without causing too much *tracking error*. Practical for *fixed income* funds based on indexes composed of thousands of *securities,* such as the *Agg*.

Savings and loan

A regulated financial institution that accepts deposits and makes *loans* primarily in the form of *mortgages*.

Scarcity bias

The mental tendency to want things that seem to be in short supply.

Second mortgage

A *loan secured* by *real estate* taken out while another loan secured by the same *property* is already in effect, as with a *home equity line of credit*.

Secured

The characteristic of a *debt* that means it's backed by a specific *asset*, as with a *mortgage*. Also called *collateralized*. The opposite of *unsecured*.

Securities and Exchange Commission

The U.S. federal *securities* markets regulator. Shortened to *SEC*.

Securities Investor Protection Corporation

A non-profit *corporation* that helps clients retrieve *assets* from *broker-dealers* that fail. Shortened to *SIPC*.

Security

A tradable financial instrument like a *stock*, *bond*, or *option*.

Security selection

The apportioning of *capital* among individual *securities* within an *asset class*.

Selection bias

The mental tendency to gauge a data set by a nonrepresentative portion of that data set.

Self-invested personal pension

A British advantaged account comparable to a *401(k)*. Shortened to *SIPP*.

Selling rate

The amount of one currency that a seller is willing to accept for a different currency. A version of an *exchange rate*, the alternatives being the *buying rate* and the *mid-market rate*.

Semiannual

Twice a year.

Settlor

The creator of a *trust*. Also called *grantor* or *trustor*.

Share

An ownership stake in a *corporation*. Also called *stock* or *equity*.

Short-term capital gain

A *capital gain* from the sale of an *asset* owned for one year or less, generally subject to a higher *tax* rate than a *long-term capital gain*.

Simple interest

Interest without *compounding*. Calculated as *interest rate* times *principal* times *term*.

Simplified employee pension individual retirement account

An advantaged account designed to finance retirement, *contributions* to which are *tax-deductible* for the employer that makes them. Shortened to *SEP IRA*.

Small capitalization stocks

Shares in companies with small *market capitalizations*, generally under $2 billion. Shortened to *small caps*.

Small caps

Shares in firms with small *market capitalizations*, generally under $2 billion. Short for *small capitalization stocks*.

Social Security benefits

Periodic payments received by older people and certain others from the Social Security Administration.

Socially responsible investing

An approach to *investing* that prioritizes ethics. Also called *SRI*. Similar to *ESG* and *impact investing*.

Soft credit inquiry

A check of a *credit report* that does not impact *credit score* and that will not appear on future credit reports. Also called a *soft pull*. The alternative to a *hard credit inquiry*.

Soft pull

A check of a *credit report* that does not impact *credit score* and that will not appear on future credit reports. Also called a *soft credit inquiry*. The alternative to a *hard pull*.

Sole proprietorship

A form of a business that is not a *corporation*, *partnership*, or other entity that is legally distinct from its owner.

Speculating

Buying an *asset* in the hope that it can be sold at a higher price, without *fundamental analysis*.

Speculative

The characteristic of a *fixed income security* indicating a general expectation that *interest* and *principal* may not be paid as promised. Also called *high-yield*, *junk*, or *non-investment grade*.

Spread

The distance between two numbers, as with the *interest rate* on a *debt* and an *index* like the *prime rate*.

Standard and Poor's

A provider of *indexes* such as the *S&P 500*. Shortened to *S&P*.

Standard deduction

A set dollar amount that reduces *taxable income*. The alternative to *itemized deductions*.

Startup

A newly-formed business.

Statement of Specified Foreign Financial Assets

An *IRS* form used to report non-U.S. financial *assets*. Also called by its form number, *8938*.

Stepped-down basis

An heir's *tax basis* in a *depreciated asset* at the time it is inherited, generally equal to *fair market value.* The opposite of *stepped-up basis.*

Stepped-up basis

An heir's *tax basis* in an *appreciated asset* at the time it is inherited, generally equal to *fair market value.* The opposite of *stepped-down basis.*

Stock

An ownership stake in a *corporation*. Also called *share* or *equity*.

Stock exchange

An organized *securities* market such as the New York Stock Exchange.

Stock option

A *security* that gives the holder the right to buy, or sell, a *stock* at a predetermined price for a specified *term*.

Stop-loss order

An investor's instruction to a *broker* to sell a *security* if its price drops to a certain level. Also called a *stop order*.

Stop order

An investor's instruction to a *broker* to sell a *security* if its price drops to a certain level. Also called a *stop-loss order*.

Strike price

The price at which an *option* may be *exercised.* Also called *exercise price*.

Subprime

Less *creditworthy*, generally quantified by a *credit score* below 620. Also used to describe a *loan* made to a less creditworthy person.

Suitability standard

A code of conduct that requires a financial professional to make recommendations that are suitable for—but not necessarily in the best interest of—a client. Weaker than the *fiduciary* standard.

Superannuation

An Australian advantaged account system comparable to a *401(k)*.

Sweep

An automatic transfer of *cash* from one account to another, as with a *CMA* that sweeps deposits into *banks*.

Switching costs

A loss of *money* or time caused by a change, such as a transition from one *financial advisor* to another.

TIN

A series of digits that identifies a taxpayer to the *IRS* and other authorities. For an individual, generally equal to a Social Security number. Short for *tax identification number*.

TTM yield

A *fund* performance ratio. The numerator equals *distributions* per share over the last 12 months. The denominator is *NAV* at the end of those 12 months. Also called *distribution yield* or *trailing 12-month yield*.

Take-home pay

An employee's *gross income* minus *withholding* and other *tax* expenses. Also called *net income*.

Target allocation

A plan to apportion set percentages of one's wealth to different *assets* or *asset classes*.

Target-date fund

A *fund* that deliberately shifts its *asset allocation* away from *stocks* and towards *fixed income securities* over time. Also called a *life-cycle fund*.

Tax

A required payment to a government, often calculated as a percentage of a larger number like *income* or purchase price.

Tax-advantaged

Tax-deferred or *tax-exempt*, often used to describe an account like an *IRA* or a *security* like a *muni*.

Tax basis

The total original purchase price of an *asset* plus items like improvements and minus items like *depreciation*. Also called *adjusted basis* or *adjusted cost basis*.

Tax bracket

A range of *incomes* to which a *tax* rate applies. Also used to refer to the top tier of a taxpayer's income.

Tax credit

An amount by which a *tax liability* is reduced. Generally more valuable to a taxpayer than a *tax deduction*.

Tax-deductible

The characteristic of an amount that means it reduces *taxable income*, as with some *contributions* to a *traditional IRA*. Often shortened to *deductible*.

Tax deduction

An amount by which *income* subject to *tax* is reduced. Generally less valuable to a taxpayer than a *tax credit*.

Tax-deferred

Not subject to *tax* until some specified time or event, as with *returns* earned inside of a *traditional IRA*.

Tax equivalent yield

The hypothetical pre-*tax yield* of a *tax-exempt fixed income security* like a *muni*. Calculated as actual yield divided by the quantity one minus the tax rate.

Tax-exempt

Never subject to *tax*.

Tax identification number

A series of digits that identifies a taxpayer to the *IRS* and other authorities. For an individual, generally equal to a Social Security number. Shortened to *TIN*.

Tax-loss harvesting

Selling an *asset* at a loss for the purpose of creating an *income tax deduction*.

Teaser rate

A temporarily low *interest* rate charged on a *borrowing* like credit card *debt*.

Term

A period of time such as the length of a *mortgage*, often measured in years. Separately, a stipulation of a contract, such as the *exercise price* of an *option*.

Term deposit

A *bank* deposit that pays a *fixed interest rate*, and that cannot be withdrawn without penalty before a set date. Also called *CD*, *certificate of deposit* or *time deposit*.

Term insurance

A type of *life insurance* that provides *coverage* for a set number of years. An alternative to *whole life insurance*.

Ticker symbol

One to five letters that represent a *listed security*.

Time deposit

A *bank* deposit that pays a *fixed interest rate*, and that cannot be withdrawn without penalty before a set date. Also called *CD*, *certificate of deposit* or *term deposit*.

Time value of money

The principle that *money* obtained now is worth more than the same amount of money obtained later.

Title

Ownership, particularly of *real estate*.

Title insurance

A *policy* with a single *premium* that calls for a *carrier* to pay for losses a homebuyer or *mortgage* lender incurs because of challenges to the ownership of a *property*.

Total return

A measure of *investment* performance that sums *appreciation*, *dividends*, *interest*, and *realized gains*.

Tracking error

The degree to which the price of an *index fund* deviates from the price of its *index*.

Traditional IRA

An advantaged account designed to finance retirement, *contributions* to which may be *tax-deductible*.

Trailing 12-month yield

A *fund* performance ratio. The numerator equals *distributions* per *share* over the last 12 months. The denominator is *NAV* at the end of those 12 months. Also called *distribution yield* or *TTM yield*.

Transfer tax

A *tax* paid on the transfer of an *asset*, such as *real estate*.

Transunion

One of the three big U.S. *credit* reporting agencies, along with *Equifax* and *Experian*.

Treasury

A sovereign *debt* obligation of the U.S. Department of the Treasury. The plural form is *Treasurys*.

Treasury bill

A Treasury with an original time to *maturity* of up to 52 weeks. Also called a *T-Bill*.

Treasury bond

A Treasury with an original time to *maturity* of over 10 years and up to 30 years.

Treasury note

A Treasury with an original time to *maturity* of between 2 and 10 years.

Trust

A legal entity established by a *grantor* to own *assets* like a home for the purpose of passing ownership to a *beneficiary* without *probate*. Also called *trust fund*.

Trust fund

A legal entity established by a *grantor* to own *assets* like a home for the purpose of passing ownership to a *beneficiary* without *probate*. Also called *trust*.

Trustee

The *fiduciary* manager of a *trust*.

Trustor

The creator of a *trust*. Also called *grantor* or *settlor*.

Turnover rate

A measure of the amount of *investment* management activity in a *fund*. Calculated as the lesser of *securities* purchased or sold over a year, divided by monthly average *net assets*; all measured in currency. Also called *turnover ratio*.

Turnover ratio

A measure of the amount of *investment* management activity in a *fund*. Calculated as the lesser of *securities* purchased or sold over a year, divided by monthly average *net assets*; all measured in currency. Also called *turnover rate*.

UGMA

A type of *custodial account* that can hold only financial *assets*, like *stocks* and *cash*. Short for *Universal Gifts to Minors Act*. An alternative to a *UTMA*.

UIT

An older kind of *fund* that raises *money* once, has a fixed lifetime, and holds the same *securities* for the duration of that lifetime. Short for *unit investment trust*.

UTMA

A type of *custodial account* that can hold any kind of *asset*. Short for *Uniform Transfers to Minors Act*. An alternative to a *UGMA*.

Umbrella insurance

Liability insurance that *covers* amounts in excess of the limits of other insurance *policies*.

Uncorrelated

Not quantitatively related, as with the price of a *stock index fund* and the *balance* in a *bank account*.

Underwater

The state of owning *property* whose market price is below the *mortgage balance*. Separately, the characteristic of an *option* that means its *exercise price* is more than the price of the *security* it can be used to buy. Also called *out-of-the-money* in that context.

Underwriter

An *insurance* company. Also called *carrier*. Relatedly, a job title within an insurance company. Separately, a financial institution that plays a lead role in an *IPO*.

Uniform Transfers to Minors Act

A type of *custodial account* that can hold any kind of *asset*. Shortened to *UTMA*. An alternative to a *UGMA*.

Unit investment trust

An older kind of *fund* that raises *money* once, has a fixed lifetime, and holds the same *securities* for the duration of that lifetime. Shortened to *UIT*.

Universal Gifts to Minors Act

A type of *custodial account* that can hold only financial *assets*, like *stocks* and *cash*. Shortened to *UGMA*. An alternative to a *UTMA*.

Universal life insurance

A type of *life insurance* that provides *coverage* during the entire life of an insured person, with *premiums* and a *death benefit* that can change more readily than with *whole life insurance*.

Unrealized

Not actualized through a sale, as in *unrealized gain*.

Unsecured

The characteristic of a *debt* that means it's not backed by specific *assets*. The opposite of *secured* or *collateralized*.

Usury

The practice of lending *money* at *interest rates* over legal or moral limits.

Utility

The usefulness of something.

Value investing

An *active* strategy that emphasizes buying *assets* at prices below worth, based on the view that prices gravitate towards worth.

Variable

Subject to change over time, as with an *interest rate*. Also called *floating*.

Variable annuity

An *investment* product offered by *insurance* companies that promises a *return* linked to *funds* selected by the *policyholder*. An alternative to a *fixed annuity* or an *indexed annuity*.

Venture capital

A segment of the *investment* management industry concerned with buying *stock* in *privately held startups*.

Vested

The characteristic of an *asset* that means that it can be used, usually because sufficient time has passed; as with a *stock option* that can be *exercised*.

Vesting period

An interval of time after which an *asset* can be used, such as the time it takes for an *RSU* to become *stock*.

Vesting schedule

A plan that applies different *vesting periods* to different units of an *asset*, as with a *stock option* grant that vests in quarters after one, two, three, and four years respectively.

Volatility

A measure of the historic changes in some number, generally price.

W-2

An *IRS* form that reports the earnings of an *employee*. Distinct from a *1099*, which reports the earnings of an *independent contractor*.

Wash sale rule

A prohibition against using a *capital loss* from the sale of *securities* as a *tax deduction* if the same or similar securities are bought within 30 days.

Wealth tax

A periodic *tax* on *net worth*.

Whole life insurance

A type of *life insurance* that provides *coverage* during the entire life of an insured person. An alternative to *term insurance*.

Will

A written document expressing how a person wants their *estate* distributed after their death.

Windfall

An unexpected arrival of wealth.

Wire transfer

Any electronic transmission of *money*.

Withholding

A portion of *gross income* remitted directly to a *tax* authority.

Wrap fee

A single price charged by an *investment* professional or firm to provide comprehensive financial services to a client, often set as a percentage of *assets under management*.

Yield

Annualized payments received from an *asset* divided by the price of that asset, as with a *fixed income security*. With *bank* accounts, *interest* divided by *balance*.

Zero-based budgeting

A spending plan that requires each expense to be justified anew. Separately, sometimes used to mean a spending plan where the difference between *income* and expenses is zero.

BIBLIOGRAPHY

Buffett, Warren E., "The Superinvestors of Graham-and-Doddsville," *Hermes*, no. 2, 1984, pp. 4–15.

Campbell, Angus. *The Sense of Wellbeing in America: Recent Patterns and Trends*. New York: McGraw-Hill, 1981.

Cialdini, Robert B. *Influence: The Psychology of Persuasion*. Revised edition. New York: Harper Business, 2006.

Granovetter, Mark S. "The Strength of Weak Ties." *American Journal of Sociology*, vol. 78, no. 6, 1973, pp. 1360–1380.

Kahn, William A. "Psychological Conditions of Personal Engagement and Disengagement at Work." *Academy of Management Journal*, vol. 33, no. 4, 1990, pp. 692–794.

Malkiel, Burton G. *A Random Walk Down Wall Street: The Time-Tested Strategy for Successful Investing*. New York: Norton, 2015.

Marshall, Kenneth Jeffrey. *Good Stocks Cheap: Value Investing with Confidence for a Lifetime of Stock Market Outperformance*. New York: McGraw-Hill, 2017.

Pyhrr, Peter A., "Zero-base budgeting," *Harvard Business Review*, vol. 48, no. 6, November-December 1970, pp. 111–21.

Stanley, Thomas J. and William D. Danko. *The Millionaire Next Door: The Surprising Secrets of America's Wealthy*. Reissue edition. Lanham, Maryland: Taylor Trade Publishing, 2010.

Tversky, Amos and Daniel Kahneman, "Availability: A Heuristic for Judging Frequency and Probability," *Cognitive Psychology* 5, no. 2, 1973, pp. 207–232.

Weeks, Michael, "Searching for Resilience," *Edelweiss Journal*, no. XX, July 7, 2021, pp. 1–6.

NOTES

PREFACE

1. Council for Economic Education, "Survey of the States," https://www.councilforeconed.org/survey-of-the-states-2020, accessed September 12, 2021.

CHAPTER 2

1. U.S. Bureau of Labor Statistics, "Consumer Price Index," https://www.bls.gov/cpi, accessed September 12, 2021.
2. Centers for Disease Control and Prevention, "Life Expectancy," https://www.cdc.gov/nchs/nvss/life-expectancy.htm, accessed September 12, 2021.

CHAPTER 4

1. Board of Governors of the Federal Reserve System, "Terms of Credit at Commercial Banks and Finance Companies," https://www.federalreserve.gov/releases/g19/HIST/cc_hist_tc_levels.html, accessed September 12, 2021.

CHAPTER 5

1. Charlotte Alter, Suyin Haynes and Justin Worland, "Time 2019 Person of the Year: Greta Thunberg," https://time.com/person-of-the-year-2019-greta-thunberg, accessed September 12, 2021.

CHAPTER 6

1. Federal Deposit Insurance Corporation, "Deposit Insurance at a Glance," https://www.fdic.gov/resources/deposit-insurance/brochures/deposits-at-a-glance, accessed September 12, 2021.

CHAPTER 10

1. Internal Revenue Service, "IRS Provides Tax Inflation Adjustments for Tax Year 2021," https://www.irs.gov/newsroom/irs-provides-tax-inflation-adjustments-for-tax-year-2021, accessed August 12, 2021.
2. State of California Franchise Tax Board, "Tax Calculator, Tables, Rates," https://www.ftb.ca.gov/file/personal/tax-calculator-tables-rates.asp, accessed September 12, 2021.
3. Internal Revenue Service, "Topic No. 409 Capital Gains and Losses," https://www.irs.gov/taxtopics/tc409, accessed September 12, 2021.
4. U.S. Centers for Medicare and Medicaid Services, "Medicare Costs at a Glance," https://www.medicare.gov/your-medicare-costs/medicare-costs-at-a-glance, accessed September 12, 2021.
5. Internal Revenue Service, "Retirement Plans FAQs Regarding 403(b) Tax-Sheltered Annuity Plans," https://www.irs.gov/retirement-plans/retirement-plans-faqs-regarding-403b-tax-sheltered-annuity-plans, accessed August 12, 2021.
6. Internal Revenue Service, "IRC 457(b) Deferred Compensation Plans," https://www.irs.gov/retirement-plans/irc-457b-deferred-compensation-plans, accessed August 12, 2021.
7. Internal Revenue Service, "Retirement Topics - Required Minimum Distributions (RMDs)," https://www.irs.gov/retirement-plans/plan-participant-employee/retirement-topics-required-minimum-distributions-rmds, accessed September 12, 2021.
8. Internal Revenue Service, "IRA FAQs - Distributions (Withdrawals)," https://www.irs.gov/retirement-plans/retirement-plans-faqs-regarding-iras-distributions-withdrawals, accessed September 12, 2021.
9. Internal Revenue Service, "Roth Comparison Chart," https://www.irs.gov/retirement-plans/roth-comparison-chart, accessed September 12, 2021.

CHAPTER 11

1. Board of Governors of the Federal Reserve System, "Terms of Credit at Commercial Banks and Finance Companies," https://www.federalreserve.gov/releases/g19/HIST/cc_hist_tc_levels.html, accessed September 12, 2021.
2. Internal Revenue Service, "Topic No. 701 Sale of Your Home," https://www.irs.gov/taxtopics/tc701, accessed September 12, 2021.

CHAPTER 12

1. Federal Housing Finance Agency, "FHFA Announces Conforming Loan Limits for 2021," https://www.fhfa.gov/Media/PublicAffairs/Pages/FHFA-Announces-Conforming-Loan-Limits-for-2021.aspx, accessed August 12, 2021.
2. Consumer Financial Protection Bureau, "What Is a Debt-To-Income Ratio? Why Is the 43% Debt-To-Income Ratio Important?" https://www.consumerfinance.gov/ask-cfpb/what-is-a-debt-to-income-ratio-why-is-the-43-debt-to-income-ratio-important-en-1791, accessed September 12, 2021.
3. Internal Revenue Service, "Publication 936 (2020), Home Mortgage Interest Deduction," https://www.irs.gov/publications/p936, accessed September 12, 2021.

CHAPTER 13

1. Federal Deposit Insurance Corporation, "Deposit Insurance at a Glance," https://www.fdic.gov/resources/deposit-insurance/brochures/deposits-at-a-glance, accessed September 12, 2021.
2. Consumer Financial Protection Bureau, "What Is A Money Market Account?" https://www.consumerfinance.gov/ask-cfpb/what-is-a-money-market-account-en-915, accessed September 12, 2021.
3. National Credit Union Administration, "Share Insurance Fund Overview," https://www.ncua.gov/support-services/share-insurance-fund, accessed September 14, 2021.
4. Actors Federal Credit Union, "Our Story," https://www.actorsfcu.com/?start=our-story, accessed September 14, 2021.

5. SchoolsFirst Federal Credit Union, "Why Join?" https://www.schoolsfirstfcu.org/wps/portal/WhyJoin, accessed September 14, 2021.
6. Lee Federal Credit Union of Washington, "About Us," http://leefcu.com/about-us, accessed September 14, 2021.
7. Richard Milne, "Coronavirus: Nordic High-Yield Bond Funds Block Withdrawals," *Financial Times*, March 22, 2020.

CHAPTER 14

1. Internal Revenue Service, "IRS Revises Publications for Tax-Exempt Bonds," https://www.irs.gov/tax-exempt-bonds/irs-revises-publications-for-tax-exempt-bonds, accessed September 14, 2021.
2. Charles Schwab Investment Management, "Schwab S&P 500 Index Fund," https://www.schwabassetmanagement.com/products/swppx, accessed August 12, 2021.
3. Financial Industry Regulatory Authority, "Frequently Asked Questions about Advertising Regulation," https://www.finra.org/rules-guidance/guidance/faqs/advertising-regulation, accessed August 12, 2021.
4. S&P Dow Jones Indices, "S&P 500 Factsheet," August 31, 2021.
5. S&P Dow Jones Indices, "S&P 500 Equal Weight Index Factsheet," August 31, 2021.
6. FTSE Russell, "Russell 3000 Index Factsheet," August 31, 2021.
7. Securities Investor Protection Corporation, "Who We Are," https://www.sipc.org/about-sipc/, accessed September 14, 2021.
8. Certified Financial Planner Board of Standards, "The Fiduciary Obligation," https://www.cfp.net/ethics/compliance-resources/2018/12/the-fiduciary-obligation, accessed September 14, 2021.

CHAPTER 15

1. Fitch Ratings, "Fitch Affirms Kaiser Foundation Health Plan's IFS Ratings at AA-; Outlook Stable," https://www.fitchratings.com/research/insurance/fitch-affirms-kaiser-foundation-health-plan-ifs-ratings-at-aa-outlook-stable-17-05-2021, May 17, 2021, accessed September 14, 2021.

2. Internal Revenue Service, "Rev. Proc. 2021-25," https://www.irs.gov/pub/irs-drop/rp-21-25.pdf, accessed September 14, 2021.
3. Ibid.

CHAPTER 16

1. Internal Revenue Service, “Estate Tax,” https://www.irs.gov/businesses/small-businesses-self-employed/estate-tax, accessed September 14, 2021.
2. Internal Revenue Service, “Table A-Unified Rate Schedule,” https://www.irs.gov/instructions/i706#idm139646240050336, accessed September 14, 2021.
3. Commonwealth of Massachusetts, “A Guide to Estate Taxes,” https://www.mass.gov/guides/a-guide-to-estate-taxes, accessed September 15, 2021.
4. Oregon Department of Revenue, “Estate Transfer Taxes and Fiduciary Income Taxes,” https://www.oregon.gov/dor/programs/individuals/pages/estate.aspx, accessed September 15, 2021.
5. New York State, “Estate Tax,” https://www.tax.ny.gov/pit/estate/etidx.htm, accessed September 15, 2021.
6. State of Hawaii - Department of Taxation, “Instructions for Form M-6,” https://files.hawaii.gov/tax/forms/2021/m6ins.pdf, https://files.hawaii.gov/tax/forms/2020/m6ins.pdf, accessed September 15, 2021.
7. Washington State Department of Revenue, “Estate Tax Tables,” https://dor.wa.gov/taxes-rates/other-taxes/estate-tax-tables, accessed September 15, 2021.
8. Internal Revenue Service, “Frequently Asked Questions on Gift Taxes,” https://www.irs.gov/businesses/small-businesses-self-employed/frequently-asked-questions-on-gift-taxes, accessed September 15, 2021.
9. Connecticut State Department of Revenue Services, “Connecticut Gift Tax,” https://portal.ct.gov/DRS/Individuals/Individual-Tax-Page/Connecticut-Gift-Tax, accessed September 15, 2021.

10. Vanguard Group, "Vanguard S&P 500 ETF (VOO)," https://investor.vanguard.com/etf/profile/VOO, accessed September 15, 2021.
11. Internal Revenue Service, "Capital Gains, Losses, and Sale of Home," https://www.irs.gov/faqs/capital-gains-losses-and-sale-of-home, accessed August 12, 2021.
12. Internal Revenue Service, "Publication 544 (2020), Sales and Other Dispositions of Assets," https://www.irs.gov/publications/p544, accessed August 12, 2021.
13. Internal Revenue Service, "About Form 706, United States Estate (and Generation-Skipping Transfer) Tax Return," https://www.irs.gov/forms-pubs/about-form-706, accessed September 15, 2021.
14. Internal Revenue Service, "Topic No. 313 Qualified Tuition Programs (QTPs)," https://www.irs.gov/taxtopics/tc313, accessed September 16, 2021.
15. National Association of State Treasurers, "What Is a 529 Plan?" https://www.collegesavings.org/what-is-529/, accessed August 12, 2021.
16. Internal Revenue Service, "Frequently Asked Questions on Gift Taxes for Nonresidents Not Citizens of the United States," https://www.irs.gov/businesses/small-businesses-self-employed/frequently-asked-questions-on-gift-taxes-for-nonresidents-not-citizens-of-the-united-states#collapseCollapsible1631733701374, accessed September 16, 2021.
17. Internal Revenue Service, "Medical Exclusion," https://www.irs.gov/instructions/i709#idm140535812787328, accessed September 16, 2021.
18. Internal Revenue Service, "Educational Exclusion," https://www.irs.gov/instructions/i709#idm140535815103632, accessed September 16, 2021.
19. State of Maryland, Office of the Register of Wills, "Maryland Estate Rules," https://registers.maryland.gov/main/publications/hints.html, accessed September 17, 2021.

20. State of Nebraska, "2020 Nebraska Tax Expenditure Report," https://revenue.nebraska.gov/sites/revenue.nebraska.gov/files/doc/research/tax-expenditure/2020_Tax_Expenditure_Report.pdf, accessed September 17, 2021.
21. State of Alaska, "Tax Types," http://tax.alaska.gov/programs/index.aspx, accessed September 17, 2021.
22. Internal Revenue Service, "What's New - Estate and Gift Tax," https://www.irs.gov/businesses/small-businesses-self-employed/whats-new-estate-and-gift-tax, accessed September 17, 2021.
23. Internal Revenue Service, "Estate and Gift Tax FAQs," https://www.irs.gov/newsroom/estate-and-gift-tax-faqs, accessed September 17, 2021.
24. Ibid.

CHAPTER 17

1. Mark S. Granovetter, "The Strength of Weak Ties," *American Journal of Sociology* 78, no. 6 (May, 1973): 1360-1380.
2. Trader Joe's, "Careers," https://www.traderjoes.com/careers, accessed August 12, 2021.
3. Internal Revenue Service, "Retirement Topics - 401(k) and Profit-Sharing Plan Contribution Limits," https://www.irs.gov/retirement-plans/plan-participant-employee/retirement-topics-401k-and-profit-sharing-plan-contribution-limits, accessed August 12, 2021.
4. Internal Revenue Service, "IRA FAQs," https://www.irs.gov/retirement-plans/retirement-plans-faqs-regarding-iras, accessed August 12, 2021.
5. Internal Revenue Service, "Income Ranges for Determining IRA Eligibility Change for 2021," https://www.irs.gov/newsroom/income-ranges-for-determining-ira-eligibility-change-for-2021, accessed August 12, 2021.
6. Internal Revenue Service, "Amount of Roth IRA Contributions That You Can Make For 2021," https://www.irs.gov/retirement-plans/amount-of-roth-ira-contributions-that-you-can-make-for-2021, accessed August 12, 2021.

7. Internal Revenue Service, "About Form 8606, Nondeductible IRAs," https://www.irs.gov/forms-pubs/about-form-8606, accessed August 12, 2021.
8. Internal Revenue Service, "IRA Year-End Reminders," https://www.irs.gov/retirement-plans/ira-year-end-reminders, accessed August 12, 2021.
9. Internal Revenue Service, "About Form 5329, Additional Taxes on Qualified Plans (Including IRAs) and Other Tax-Favored Accounts," https://www.irs.gov/forms-pubs/about-form-5329, accessed August 12, 2021.
10. Internal Revenue Service, "Rollovers of Retirement Plan and IRA Distributions," https://www.irs.gov/retirement-plans/plan-participant-employee/rollovers-of-retirement-plan-and-ira-distributions, accessed August 12, 2021.
11. Internal Revenue Service, "SEP Contribution Limits (Including Grandfathered SARSEPs)," https://www.irs.gov/retirement-plans/plan-participant-employee/sep-contribution-limits-including-grandfathered-sarseps, accessed August 12, 2021.
12. Internal Revenue Service, "SEP Plan FAQs," https://www.irs.gov/retirement-plans/retirement-plans-faqs-regarding-seps, accessed August 12, 2021.

CHAPTER 18

1. Internal Revenue Service, "Topic No. 701 Sale of Your Home," https://www.irs.gov/taxtopics/tc701, accessed September 17, 2021.
2. Internal Revenue Service, "Topic No. 415 Renting Residential and Vacation Property," https://www.irs.gov/taxtopics/tc415, accessed September 17, 2021.

CHAPTER 19

1. Consumer Financial Protection Bureau, "Will Requesting My Credit Report Hurt My Credit Score?" https://www.consumerfinance.gov/ask-cfpb/will-requesting-my-credit-report-hurt-my-credit-score-en-1229, accessed September 17, 2021.

2. Consumer Financial Protection Bureau, "What exactly happens when a mortgage lender checks my credit?" https://www.consumerfinance.gov/ask-cfpb/what-exactly-happens-when-a-mortgage-lender-checks-my-credit-en-2005/, accessed September 17, 2021.
3. Internal Revenue Service, "Topic No. 504 Home Mortgage Points," https://www.irs.gov/taxtopics/tc504, accessed September 17, 2021.

CHAPTER 20

1. EmigrantDirect, "Open Savings Account Online - Learn More," https://www.emigrantdirect.com/securebanking/learnMore.do, accessed September 19, 2021.
2. Federal Deposit Insurance Corporation, "Your Insured Deposits," https://www.fdic.gov/resources/deposit-insurance/brochures/insured-deposits, accessed September 19, 2021.
3. U.S. Department of the Treasury, "Is Savings Bond Interest Taxable?" https://www.treasurydirect.gov/indiv/research/indepth/ibonds/res_ibonds_itaxconsider.htm#tax, accessed September 19, 2021.
4. Internal Revenue Service, "About Form 8938, Statement of Specified Foreign Financial Assets," https://www.irs.gov/forms-pubs/about-form-8938, accessed September 19, 2021.

CHAPTER 21

1. S&P Dow Jones Indices, "S&P 500 Growth," https://www.spglobal.com/spdji/en/idsenhancedfactsheet/file.pdf?calcFrequency=M&force_download=true&hostIdentifier=48190c8c-42c4-46af-8d1a-0cd5db894797&indexId=2029, accessed September 19, 2021.
2. S&P Dow Jones Indices, "S&P SmallCap 600 Growth," https://www.spglobal.com/spdji/en/idsenhancedfactsheet/file.pdf?calcFrequency=M&force_download=true&hostIdentifier=48190c8c-42c4-46af-8d1a-0cd5db894797&indexId=2240, accessed September 19, 2021.

3. Vanguard Group, "Vanguard ETFs," https://investor.vanguard.com/etf/list#/etf/name/month-end-returns, accessed September 19, 2021.
4. S&P Dow Jones Indices, "S&P SmallCap 600 Growth," https://www.spglobal.com/spdji/en/idsenhancedfactsheet/file.pdf?calcFrequency=M&force_download=true&hostIdentifier=48190c8c-42c4-46af-8d1a-0cd5db894797&indexId=2240, accessed September 19, 2021.
5. FTSE Russell, "FTSE U.S. All Cap Choice Index," https://research.ftserussell.com/Analytics/FactSheets/Home/DownloadSingleIssue?openfile=open&issueName=FGCUSAC&isManual=False, accessed September 19, 2021.
6. Ibid.
7. Georgia Wells, Jeff Horwitz, and Deepa Seetharaman, "Facebook Knows Instagram Is Toxic for Teen Girls, Company Documents Show," *The Wall Street Journal*, September 14, 2021.
8. Jack Nicas and Kellen Browning, "Tim Cook Faces Surprising Employee Unrest at Apple," *The New York Times*, September 17, 2021.
9. JPMorgan Chase & Co., *Schedule 14A*, April 7, 2021.
10. Internal Revenue Service, "Retirement Plan and IRA Required Minimum Distributions FAQs," https://www.irs.gov/retirement-plans/retirement-plans-faqs-regarding-required-minimum-distributions, accessed September 19, 2021.
11. United States Social Security Administration, "Income Taxes And Your Social Security Benefit," https://www.ssa.gov/benefits/retirement/planner/taxes.html, accessed September 19, 2021.
12. Vanguard Group, "VBMFX," https://institutional.vanguard.com/web/c1/investments/product-details/fund/0084, accessed September 19, 2021.
13. Bloomberg L.P., "Bloomberg Barclays U.S. Agg Total Return Value Unhedged USD," https://www.bloomberg.com/quote/LBUSTRUU:IND, accessed September 19, 2021.

14. Vanguard Group, "Vanguard Total Bond Market ETF (BND)," https://investor.vanguard.com/etf/profile/overview/bnd, accessed August 12, 2021.
15. U.S. Securities and Exchange Commission, "Municipal Bonds," https://www.investor.gov/introduction-investing/investing-basics/investment-products/bonds-or-fixed-income-products-0, accessed September 19, 2021.
16. Vanguard Group, "Vanguard Mutual Funds," https://investor.vanguard.com/mutual-funds/list?assetclass=bond&taxeff=xmpt#/mutual-funds/asset-class/month-end-returns, accessed September 19, 2021.
17. Vanguard Group, "Vanguard New York Long-Term Tax-Exempt Fund Admiral Shares (VNYUX)," https://investor.vanguard.com/mutual-funds/profile/overview/vnyux, accessed September 19, 2021.
18. Vanguard Group, "Vanguard Intermediate-Term Tax-Exempt Fund Admiral Shares (VWIUX)," https://investor.vanguard.com/mutual-funds/profile/overview/vwiux, accessed September 19, 2021.
19. Internal Revenue Service, "Retirement Plan and IRA Required Minimum Distributions FAQs," https://www.irs.gov/retirement-plans/retirement-plans-faqs-regarding-required-minimum-distributions, accessed September 19, 2021.
20. Internal Revenue Service, "Publication 550 (2020), Investment Income and Expenses," https://www.irs.gov/publications/p550, accessed August 12, 2021.

CHAPTER 22

1. U.S. Centers for Medicare and Medicaid Services, "Get the Basics," https://www.medicare.gov/sign-up-change-plans/get-started-with-medicare/get-the-basics, accessed August 12, 2021.

CHAPTER 23

1. Internal Revenue Service, "IRS Provides Tax Inflation Adjustments for Tax Year 2021," https://www.irs.gov/newsroom/irs-provides-tax-inflation-adjustments-for-tax-year-2021, accessed August 12, 2021.

2. Internal Revenue Service, "Frequently Asked Questions on Gift Taxes," https://www.irs.gov/businesses/small-businesses-self-employed/frequently-asked-questions-on-gift-taxes, accessed August 12, 2021.
3. Internal Revenue Service, "Treasury, IRS: Making Large Gifts Now Won't Harm Estates After 2025," https://www.irs.gov/newsroom/treasury-irs-making-large-gifts-now-wont-harm-estates-after-2025, accessed September 19, 2021.
4. Internal Revenue Service, "Topic No. 313 Qualified Tuition Programs (QTPs)," https://www.irs.gov/taxtopics/tc313, accessed September 19, 2021.
5. Internal Revenue Service, "About Form 706, United States Estate (and Generation-Skipping Transfer) Tax Return," https://www.irs.gov/forms-pubs/about-form-706, accessed September 19, 2021.
6. S&P Dow Jones Indices, "Index Dashboard: S&P 500 Factor Indices," https://www.spglobal.com/spdji/en/documents/commentary/dashboard-sp-500-factor-2020-01.pdf?force_download=true, accessed September 19, 2021.

INDEX

ABOUT THE AUTHOR

Kenneth Jeffrey Marshall is an author, professor, and value investor. He teaches personal finance and value investing at Stanford University; industry analysis in the masters in engineering leadership program at the University of California, Berkeley; and value investing in the masters in finance program at the Stockholm School of Economics. He is the author of the 2017 book *Good Stocks Cheap: Value Investing with Confidence for a Lifetime of Stock Market Outperformance*, which in 2019 was also published in Chinese. He holds a BA in Economics, International Area Studies from the University of California, Los Angeles; and an MBA from Harvard University.

www.kennethjeffreymarshall.com

CPSIA information can be obtained
at www.ICGtesting.com
Printed in the USA
FSHW011300111121
86154FS

9 781737 673408